£.85

W. G. Downie

All Saints Vicarage

Grays.

PREACHING
IN THEORY AND PRACTICE

PREACHING
IN THEORY AND PRACTICE

By the Rev.
SAMUEL McCOMB, D.D.

WITH AN INTRODUCTION
By the Rev.
HARRY EMERSON FOSDICK, D.D.

NEW YORK
OXFORD UNIVERSITY PRESS
AMERICAN BRANCH: 35 WEST 32ND STREET
LONDON, TORONTO, MELBOURNE & BOMBAY
1926

To
the Memory of
FREDERICK WILLIAM ROBERTSON
GEORGE MacDONALD
AND
STOPFORD AUGUSTUS BROOKE
MASTERS OF THE ART OF PREACHING
IN HUMBLE ACKNOWLEDGMENT
OF A LIFE-LONG DEBT

PREFATORY NOTE

THE substance of the chapters of this book was delivered as lectures to students preparing for the ministry at the Episcopal Theological School, Cambridge, 1921–1924. Since the original draft of the lectures was written the lives of two eminent preachers have appeared, Dr. J. H. Jowett and Bishop W. Boyd Carpenter. On these I have drawn for illustrations of what I hold to be the true principles of modern preaching.

My thanks are due and are hereby tendered to my friends, Professor William McDougall, of Harvard University, and Principal H. D. A. Major, Ripon Hall, Oxford, for their kindness in reading portions of the manuscript and for their valuable suggestions.

The book has, of course, no pretension to be an exhaustive treatise in the science of homiletics. Nor has it anything to say to those who have had considerable practice in the art of preaching. It simply seeks to emphasize the essentials, and it is intended for students and younger ministers who are looking for help in the practice of the most difficult of all arts.

The Chapter on "The Psychology of Preaching — I. The Preacher" appeared in *The Modern Churchman* for January, 1926. Thanks are hereby tendered the Editor and Publisher for their kind permission to reprint.

CONTENTS

INTRODUCTION

By HARRY EMERSON FOSDICK, D.D.

THESE lectures of Dr. McComb are a welcome addition to the new literature on preaching. The more so because preaching has fallen on dangerous days when many folk are critically doubtful of its present or future usefulness. That Protestantism has trusted too largely to the quantity of its preaching seems plain. It has commonly deluged its devotees with sermons, played spendthrift with formal religious discourses to the great detriment of their quality and the great boredom of many of their hearers. We need not be surprised, therefore, at the present revulsion against preaching. We have richly deserved it. We have preached too much and not well enough. We need less quantity and more quality. The homiletical currency has been badly overinflated and we need a return to the gold standard.

These lectures are an endeavor to encourage that movement, to make preaching seem what it really is — a weighty responsibility, a fine art, an indispensable social function, a sacred entrustment of influence. When preaching is taken so seri-

ously there will be an inevitable tendency to make
what we do of it better, even if we have to do
less.

The work of the preacher is being seriously
affected by the profound changes going on in the
mind of the modern world. The days of dogmatic and authoritarian proclamation from the
pulpit are ended for intelligent audiences. Even
propaganda, in its milder senses, is suspect, and to
be a salaried propagandist for a foregone conclusion, as the preacher is commonly supposed to be,
is to occupy a position whose influence is undercut
to start with. Every wise preacher will take this
new mood seriously into account. It will provoke
him to humility and searching of heart. It will
despoil him of scribal pretense and will send him
to his sermon on Sunday with a method of approach to his hearers very different from that
which authoritarian pulpiteers commonly use.
The psychologists call it the " project method "
and the prescription for it can be briefly put: start
with a live issue, a real problem, personal or
social, perplexing to the mind or disturbing to
the conscience of the people; face that problem
fairly, deal with it honestly, and throw such light
on it from the Spirit of Christ that the people
will go out able to think more clearly and live
more nobly because of that sermon's illumination.
That is real preaching, and not only has such

preaching not been outgrown, but there are few things that modern folk are hungrier for than that.

These lectures of Dr. McComb are a valuable contribution to that kind of work and notably in such chapters as those on "The Psychology of Preaching" he has given wise guidance and stimulating counsel for us all.

PREACHING IN THEORY AND PRACTICE

I

THE PLACE OF THE PULPIT IN THE MODERN WORLD

EVERYBODY knows that the preacher has fallen on evil days. Sermons are flat, dull, uninteresting, out of relation to the needs of the age, sentimental, over-intellectual or not intellectual enough, platitudinous, impotent, devoid of human appeal.

Doubtless these things have been said about some sermons ever since the preacher appeared among men. But now a new note is heard. Critics both within and without the Church assure us that preaching has been over-rated, that its day is over, and that the sooner it is recognized as a superfluity — so much excess baggage in the religious life — the better it will be for all concerned.

"I think you are all gone mad about preaching," says one of the interlocutors in Canon Twells's charming "Colloquies on Preaching." "You vastly overrate its importance and possible influence. A ten minutes' composition with no heresy in it, and a few nice quotations from the early fathers surely satisfies every reasonable requirement. . . . I could almost wish the custom of pre-Reformation times could be adopted again; no sermon, as a general rule, but now and then a preaching friar coming around as a treat."

From within the religious realm we hear voices assuring us that one of the causes of the decline in churchgoing is the sermon. Abolish the pulpit, emphasise the artistic and aesthetic elements in worship, glorify the sacramental and ceremonial side of worship, and people will be won back to the services of the Church and find in them their highest delight. Indeed the sermon is a foreign element, intruding incongruously into the sphere of worship. But the effort to magnify the sacramental and the ritualistic by making light of the prophetic element in the devotional life is doomed to failure. Men will insist in trying to understand what religion really means. Consistent and effective action is born of deep convictions, and convictions are the fruit only of a principle grasped by the intelligence. The Russian Church has consistently neglected preaching; Scotland has as consistently cultivated it. The contrasted moral phenomena of Russia and Scotland receive, in part, their explanation here. But indeed there is no incongruity between the devotion created by Christ's presence in the Sacrament and Prayer and

His presence in the Word as preached. Every true sermon is or ought to be steeped in the spirit of worship. Is it not the aim of the preacher who understands his task, to evoke from his hearers sorrow for past wrongdoing, new resolutions for the future, a throwing of themselves upon the Divine mercy and an earnest aspiration after higher things? And are not these states of soul such as imply a worshipful attitude? Doubtless there is a difference between the mental state of one engaged in prayer and that of one listening to a sermon, but the difference need not develop into incompatibility.

Other critics of the pulpit contend that the spread of education, the production of books and magazines, more particularly the novel and the drama, have eclipsed the work and usefulness of preaching. Any intelligent man with the help of a concordance and a Bible dictionary can master the contents of Scripture and know it as well as any trained pulpit speaker. The contention argues a strange misconception of the function of preaching. The preacher is concerned with religion and the ultimate values of the spiritual life, not primarily with information about the Bible. The Bible and theology can be used as a means to an end, and the end is the interpretation of life. They are the instruments which the preacher uses but they do not constitute his specific task. Nor can the novelist or the dramatist discharge that task instead of him. They hold up the mirror to life, and reveal the secret motives of men in all their subtle and complicated workings. Shakespeare and Balzac and Tolstoi are masters in the knowledge of the natural man, but we must go elsewhere to hear about the spiritual man, the character of God, and the relations between the divine and the human. In brief, the preacher has a Gospel based, as he believes, on a revelation of the transcendental world and equipped with power to transform and save the individual and the race. This fact puts him in a category by himself. His work cannot be transferred to any other workman. If he does not do it, then it is not done.

Still further: not only has he a Gospel, but it is a Gospel which, presumably, he has himself experienced. The vital element in preaching is not the ideas set forth; it is the transmission of that mysterious, elusive, indefinable something which we call personality. Of this something we can only say, it is God-given, and it is through it that the truth reaches the heart and conquers the will. Hence neither book nor sacrament nor ceremony can ever take the place of the living breathing man who utters the message of the Eternal in his own way and as he himself has felt its subduing and transforming power. Hence the noble prophecies of two of the most renowned of preachers: —

" The world has not heard its best preaching yet. If there is more of God's truth for men to know, and if it is possible for the men who utter it to become more pure and godly, then, with both of its elements more complete than they have ever been before, preaching must some day be a complete power. But that better preaching will not come by any sudden leap of inspiration. As the preaching of the present came from the preaching of the past, so the preaching that is to be will come from the preaching that is now." [1] " True preaching is yet to come," said Beecher. " Of all professions for young men to look forward to I do not know of another one that seems to me to have such scope before it in the future as preaching. There is one fact that is not going to be overturned by science; and that is: the necessity of human development and the capacity there is in man of being opened up and improved. . . . If there is one thing more worthy of being worked for than another, it is the human soul." [2]

While believing therefore, that preaching, so far from being obsolete, has really its great days before it, I nevertheless agree that much preaching today leaves the hearers cold, and the question is, Why? Mainly because many preachers have no real vision and therefore no real under-

[1] Phillips Brooks: *Lectures on Preaching*, pp. 33–34.
[2] *Yale Lectures*, p. 20.

standing of the times. They are still living in the past. They do not glimpse the astounding truth that mankind is passing through the agonies of the greatest upheaval of thought against traditionalism in all its forms the world has ever witnessed. Now religion is man's most real, most universal possession, and therefore in this sphere reformation is slowest because always in conflict with the native inertia of human nature. Yet the young are here and refuse to tolerate this conservatism. They have broken definitely with the past so dear to older people, and they are forsaking our churches simply because the preacher does not appear to understand them or sympathize with what they feel and feel keenly. To them our services and our sermons seem the most spectral of inanities. The force of tradition draws still a number of older persons to the churches, but the mass for which that tradition has long since lost its meaning, turns away in sheer indifference. Yet the spiritual revival will take place, and as Dr. L. P. Jacks points out in his " Lost Radiance of the Christian Religion," if the pulpit cannot do its duty effectively, the modern educationist by including religion and ethics in the first place in his curriculum, will replace the preacher. What, then, is to be done?

The preacher must gain a new and compelling vision of the age, and a new and compelling sense

of the power of his message. He must get face
to face with the real forces of his time, and proclaim his message in terms that can be understood,
that are relevant to the living issues of his age.
To use the favorite phrase of the late Professor
Sanday he must illustrate in his teaching "con-
tinuity of thought with relativity of expression."
He must sympathize with the yearnings and dis-
satisfaction of multitudes who have outgrown the
religion of their childhood and who are out for a
new and living word to meet their spiritual needs.
It has been said of Basil Wilberforce that he gave
his hearers something new and satisfied them; and
then they found that what he had given them was
nothing new at all, but just the old truths adapted
to modern requirements.

What, then, are the conditions of the age to
which the preacher must address himself?

It goes without saying that our age is nothing
if not critical. Educated men have a deep-rooted
distrust of statements that are merely traditional.
The authenticity and inspiration of the Bible to
which at one time the preacher could appeal, conscious that his audience was with him, have been
in their traditional form, undermined. His
hearers doubt whether the preacher knows more
than anybody else about the questions that he
discusses so easily. The only thing many feel
they can be sure of is the work of science, and

science is dumb on all the really vital questions. What, then, is the preacher to do? To begin with: he must acknowledge that there are realms where a wise agnosticism is the only fitting attitude for the finite spirit. The inner life of the Godhead, the pre-existence of souls, the nature of the world beyond the grave, the reconciliation of moral freedom with inviolable law — these and other problems must be frankly acknowledged to be insoluble. And men will all the more easily re-sign themselves to permanent ignorance in these matters, if they are made to see that life and the necessities of life are quite independent of such questionings. If philosophy has done nothing else, it has at least established the limitations of man's power to know. Again and again in various avenues of investigation, there is written up the notice: " No Thoroughfare."

But the preacher who would influence the mod-ern hearers will, while relegating metaphysical questions to the schools, bring into prominence the truths of history and experience. And in doing so he will distinguish between the trivial and the important, the accidental and the essential. The main weakness of the modern pulpit — apart from notable exceptions — is the confusion between what is vital to the interests of the spiritual life and what is purely external. The questions which have recently tormented large sections of the religious public in the furious debate between modernists and fundamentalists would never have arisen if the Christian pulpit had done its duty as a teaching institute. What are we to say of the appalling ignorance of those who deny the name of Christian to their brothers who are unable to see any real connection between the Virgin-birth of Jesus and the Incarnation? The Virgin-birth may be or may not be an historical fact. The evidence is too scanty to compel assent. Is it credible that the Providence which rules in history would make the spiritual interests of humanity depend on a doubtful happening in time? In a word, where there are so many difficulties, the preacher is doing ill service to his fellows by failing to remove such as appear quite superfluous.

Or take the other stumbling block in the way of many to a living faith in Christianity, the story of the physical resurrection of Jesus. A theological professor addressing his students recently put this question to which of course he expected an affirmative reply: " Did His (Christ's) crucified body come forth from the grave in resurrection form? " And he went on to say: " Certain good Christian doctrines are inevitable if the facts are recognized. To deny the facts themselves is to revolutionize Christianity." [3] And among these facts he put the alleged fact of the physical resurrection of the

<hr />

[3] Mullins: *Christianity at the Crossroads*, p. 29.

Saviour. How many Easter services are ruined by this misunderstanding! How many earnest minds are needlessly perplexed! It is the duty of the preacher to bring relief to these by showing that, whatever evidence may be adduced for the Empty Tomb, faith in a risen and victorious Christ does not rest upon it, but upon something more inward and personal. Here the appeal must be to experience. The essence of the Resurrection faith does not lie in the tradition that the body of Jesus was miraculously restored to life, but in a present realization of One who is alive and energizes in every heart that is open to His influence. This was unquestionably the generative cause of the faith of the early disciples. Though it cannot be doubted that he appeared to them after His death (possibly by some method hinted at in the phenomena of telepathy) and convinced them of His continued existence — " I live yet not I but Christ liveth in me." When the Apostle uttered those words he was lifted into a realm where physical or sensuous happenings seemed the merest irrelevance.

When the preacher once more strikes the note of truth and reality men will crowd to hear him. The pulpit which today has so largely lost its power will enter on an era of unprecedented influence and will renew its ancient triumphs. A very wise man has said that " there is nothing by which more good might be done than by good preaching. I mean chiefly: (1) The connection of religion with life, (2) The assertion of a regard for truth as a part of religious duty — the spirit of truth." [4]

So far the preacher's concern will have been with men anxious to believe but embarrassed and hindered by the growths of tradition. What of the "intellectuals" who frankly dismiss all religion as a superstition thus holding man back from the realization of his nature? Fundamentalists and modernists alike are, we are now told, the victims of a sort of "reaction of defence" against the pressure of fate, the precarious hold man has on existence. Such ideas as God, the soul, immortality, — have nothing corresponding to them among the realities of the universe. They can be psychologically explained. They are the product of dreams and are "such stuff as dreams are made of." It is on this field of battle that the claims of the Christian religion will be ultimately fought out, and the struggle will be more vital to man's spiritual interests than even the Great War to his political interests. It will be a life and death conflict. What part has the preacher to play in it? The promise of victory is not to the defender but to the attacker. Let him boldly challenge the presuppositions of the naturalists. Is man really what

---

[4] *Benjamin Jowett's Life and Letters,* Vol. I, p. 272.

the naturalists imagine him to be? The question can be answered only by an appeal to history and experience. Has man ever found peace, a motive for life and work, in a naturalistic conception of himself? On the contrary, has not man, worsted in the struggle for existence, baffled and disillusioned by poignant experiences, turned to an ever-living Presence, to find his energies re-vitalized, his strength reinforced, and his mental and spiritual outlook vastly expanded? Can psychology explain away the permanent needs of human nature and the satisfaction of those needs through contact with an objective spiritual world? This would be to go beyond its province, which is only concerned with the description of mental processes, states and activities. If psychology cannot prove God, neither can it disprove Him.

There is another condition under which the preacher must perform his task today. The age is marked by a profound social unrest. This is not a local phenomenon, —it is racial, world wide. The proletariat of the East as well as of the West has arisen to shake the thrones of privilege and power. Everywhere among Christians and non-Christians alike a spirit of discontent and restlessness is abroad. How stands the preacher, confronted as he is with a confusion of facts and theories and social doctrines unprecedented in the history of mankind? It is too late in the day to apologize for the Gospel as a message to society as well as to the individual. The very phrase, " Kingdom of God," so fundamental in Christ's teaching, proved that His mission was to achieve social as well as personal reconstruction. Christ knew that man needed physical sustenance as well as spiritual. He includes in his model prayer a petition for daily bread; but he takes care to put the prayer for the kingdom *before* this petition. His own words interpret this order: " Seek ye first the kingdom of God and its righteousness and all these things shall be added unto you." This means that Jesus was first and foremost a spiritual idealist, and only in a subordinate fashion " an economic realist." Still, He deals with man as a whole, body and soul, and His followers are beginning to understand Him here. Even preachers whose message is preëminently individualistic insist that it is the duty of the Christian pulpit to champion the cause of the poor and the oppressed, to lift up its voice against moral and social evils and to spare not. But what is to be the preacher's attitude towards the claims of organized labor? What has he to say about socio-economic questions that agitate the minds of the wage-earning classes, such as the equable distribution of wealth, the nationalization of private enterprises, the standard of a living wage, the restrictions of hours of work, the adjustment of prices of commodities. Can there be an effective social message from the pulpit without the passing of judgment on these questions?

On the one hand, it cannot be denied that the preacher is suspect to the laborite, speaking as he does from a position which he holds by the favor of the well-to-do classes. On the other hand, unless he is an expert in economic science, his utterances on these problems are bound to be worthless and even mischievous. Conscious of this dilemma, many preachers ignore the social teaching of the Gospel and thereby cut themselves off from a wide realm of the life of their time; they fall back upon such generalities as the Fatherhood of God and the brotherhood of man, ideas which if utilized would indeed dissipate all the ills of the social order! Such thoughts, however eloquently expressed, effect nothing. They belong to one sphere, the concrete situation belongs to another. They can inspire, and energize the man who opens mind and heart to their power, but they cannot solve a single scientific problem. Never let the preacher forget that economic questions are scientific questions and can be solved only by scientific means. The need here is primarily for the head and not the heart, and the hour will come when men of financial genius will consecrate not only their money but their intellect also to the service of the kingdom, and will work out an economic scheme under which God's children will be able to live and work in happiness and peace. Much preaching of the Social Gospel has been a failure by reason of the neglect of this simple principle. If a preacher has the technical knowledge and the necessary skill in presenting it, he can do splendid service in bringing opposed classes together on the basis of right reason. But such a man is quite exceptional. The great majority of preachers have no such knowledge, and when they dogmatize on matters of which they have a mere amateur's information they talk irritating twaddle.

Nevertheless there is a field where the preacher is within his rights. He can stir his own conscience and the consciences of his hearers upon the conditions of the present social order. Are we living under a *régime* that tends to embody the will of God or that in not a few ways tends to illustrate the power of the Devil? Once he is convinced that great masses of his fellowmen are living under the rule of injustice, and assuming that this conviction is born of painstaking study, he can urge upon his hearers the duty of inquiry, of patient, unselfish effort to get at the facts; he can proclaim with words that flame that only justice can save the world from revolution. Nor are there lacking lurid illustrations in contemporary history to back up his assertions. Let the preacher but master the fundamental principles of Christ's teaching and then dispassionately view the modern industrial system in this light. He will not cease to enforce the great truths of personal religion, the Love of God, forgiveness, conversion, the new life, immortality, the Lordship of Christ, but he will so preach them that they will inevitably lead to a passion for social reform and social reconstruction. His preaching will render it plain that the sincerity of personal faith can be judged by the effectiveness of the believer's social service. Men go to Christ for a definite law to decide their difficult questions. He refuses to give them what they ask. His respect for human personality is too great to permit Him to treat them like children. But he lays down eternal principles on which alone can be safely built the structure of life, personal, social, commercial, national and international. The task before the modern preacher is to call upon men to apply these principles to the concrete issues of the hour. And he may strengthen himself with the reflection that the preaching of Christ and His religion has seen its grandest triumphs invariably in periods of decadence, corruption and revolt. Here as elsewhere it remains true that " history is the best cordial for drooping spirits."

II

PREPARATION FOR PREACHING

I. General Preparation

Paradoxical as it sounds, "the less special preparation that is needed for a sermon, the better the sermon is." And the reason is that the sermon in that case rests on the solid acquirements of a disciplined mind, not on the information gathered for the needs of the moment and therefore without vital relations to the growth of the personal life. Someone has humorously said that the only way to preach well is to begin ten years ago. It is a cramping and petty aim to be concentrating all our available energies on preparing the sermon for the following Sunday. No inconsiderable portion of a preacher's time should be spent in general intellectual self-culture; because as the preacher is, such is the sermon. Many preachers feel that the burden of preparing one or two fresh discourses every week is almost intolerable. On enquiry it will be found that these men have been occupied with matters that have not made them ready for the task of preparing a discourse with a sense of ease and mastery. It is out of a trained and disciplined nature that a real sermon, a living word, comes forth armed with power to convince the intellect, kindle the imagination and carry the will by storm. The hearer feels that he is in the presence of a very reservoir of reserve force.

What, then, are the chief means of spiritual self-culture with a view to the work of the pulpit?

1. The Study of the Bible

The Bible, or the most of it, is in closest contact with life, and it is this quality which makes it the most powerful weapon in the preacher's arsenal. Its contents have come through the experience of men. It matters little whether we call it "revelation" or "discovery"; that depends on whether we view it from the divine or human point of view. What is discovered must have first existed. How could the truth be found if it were not already there? Here, then, is a storehouse of religious thought and experience and aspiration on whose resources we are to draw for the illumination and guidance of our hearers. Our first business is therefore to know it, to know *it*, I repeat, not merely books *about* it. This work of mastering the Bible is the task of a lifetime. When we have done our best there is still more light to break forth from the Word. For this book, or rather library, is not a finished product, it is a living spirit revealing new truths to meet new occasions. The lofty oratory of Isaiah, the parables of Jesus, the sermons of Peter, the letters of Paul, — all bear the mark of life-experiences and imply an environment and background which must be known if the spiritual messages issuing out of them are to be understood. We should study the Bible book by book, examining each in the light of the fundamental aim of the writer. And here, I believe, certain books should be selected for specially arduous study and research so that eventually you may without undue lack of modesty regard yourself as an authority upon the particular parts of Scripture you have chosen as your province.

Still further, the great personalities of the Bible call for patient and sympathic study. Abraham, Joseph, Moses, Samuel, David, Elijah, Jeremiah, Ezekiel, Nehemiah, John the Baptist, Peter, Paul, and above all the divine Man who is the centre of the world to which these belong — all these are to be studied and not only studied but lived with as flesh and blood realities.

But this is not all. The knowledge of the Bible which the preacher requires is not merely acquaintance with the earthen vessels in which the treasure is borne to us, but an inner apprehension, a vital appropriation of the treasure itself. Following out a suggestion of one of the Yale lectures on preaching, every preacher would do well to have at least three Bibles, one for the critical and historical knowledge of the text, another for a knowledge of the religious and theological ideas of the various writers, and a third for a devotional and personal subjection of heart and mind to the inspirations of the Spirit of holiness that speaks through the book, now in a less, and now in a greater degree. There is a danger against which the preacher must resolutely guard himself, that of regarding the Bible simply and solely as a mere tool of a profession, a storehouse of homiletic material. The nemesis of thinness and superficiality is bound to overtake such a utilitarian habit.

2. The Study of the Great Men and Movements in the History of the Church

Mental stimulus and spiritual help must come from contact with men like Augustine, Francis of Assisi, Luther, Erasmus, Wesley, Fox and many another mystic and reformer and thinker. Christianity was not completed with the New Testament. From Christ there streams an ever-living force which incarnates itself in illustrious spirits for the refreshment and revitalizing of each successive age. Hence in knowing these men, we know Christ, we share a portion of the unsearchable riches of His wisdom and goodness. There are certain self-revealing books which every preacher ought to make his own. Among them let me name, Augustine's *Confessions*, Luther's *Table-talk*, the *Journals* of Wesley, Woolman, Amiel, and Tolstoi. Such movements of religious thought as the revival of religion in the thirteenth century, the Reformation, the Cambridge Platonist movement in the seventeenth century, the Evangelical Revival, the Oxford movement, the Liberal movement of the nineteenth century, the Modernist movement of our own time, with their various contributions to Christian thought and life, demand careful understanding and appreciation. Failure to do justice to those elements of truth that are to be discovered in theories and tendencies with which we may have but scant sympathy means a loss of influence, inability to win men to what we believe to be a more adequate apprehension of the truth. There is no better safeguard against intolerance and partisanship than a wide and sympathetic knowledge of Christian history and of the great men who have worked there. And what about movements of thought in our own time? Shall we allow our prejudices to blind us to the contributions which these may bring to religion and the higher life of man? Even such unconventional activities as those of Psychical Research, Christian Science, New

Thought and allied phases deserve not condemnation but understanding. Some truth may be there, why not have it and use it?

But even for the actual work of preaching, the history of the Church provides a wealthy mine of illustrative material. The dramatic situations, the pregnant, sententious sayings struck out in the heat of conflict, the illustrations of the graces and virtues of Christ shining forth in the lives of heroic men and women, the mighty contrasts between greatness and littleness, nobility and baseness, faith and unbelief of which history is full — all these can give reality and convincing force to the preacher's argument. One of the best examples of how such knowledge can be made available for instruction and encouragement is to be found in a sermon by Julius Hare in his "Victory of Faith." He is preaching from the text, "Who is he that overcometh the world but he who believeth that Jesus is the Son of God?" and proceeds to illustrate the power of faith by recording some of its "great achievements." [1]

By faith Paul called the nations to the knowledge of Christ. . . .

By faith he stood before Felix, Festus and Agrippa.

By faith Polycarp, when above ninety years old,

[1] Pp. 225–232. The passage is too long for quotations in full; only a short portion is given here.

being commanded to revile Christ, with the promise that he should be set free, replied, " Eighty and six years have I served Him; and He has done me no wrong. How can I blaspheme my King who has saved me? "

By faith Ambrose preserved the churches of Milan from the Arian Empress and her Gothic soldiers. . . .

By faith Chrystostom, when deposed, an aged exile, in a remote savage land, assailed by all manner of sufferings, still watched on, exhorted and comforted his Church at Constantinople. . . .

By faith Boniface, leaving his home and refusing high ecclesiastical honors, went into the wilds of Germany to convert the heathen natives. . . .

By faith the Waldensians retired among the mountain fastnesses, and dwelt in the caves of the Alps, that they might keep their religion in undefiled purity. . . .

By faith Wycliffe, the morning star of the Reformation, rose out of the darkness, and heralded the coming daylight.

By faith Luther proclaimed his Theses against the doctrine of Indulgence. By faith he went to the diet of Worms though warned that the fate of Hus would await him, going in the strength of Christ, in despite of the gates of hell, and of the Prince of the powers of the air. . . .

By faith the noble army of Martyrs mounted in their fiery chariots to heaven.

By faith Oberlin went forth among the Vosges and spread the blessings of religion and civilization among the wild inhabitants.

By faith Clarkson and Wilberforce overthrew the slave trade. . . .

And what shall I say more? For the time would fail me to tell of Ignatius and Justin and Cyprian and Tertullian and Basil and Augustine and Patrick and Columba and Bede and Anselm and Hus and Melanchthon and Zwingli and Knox and Calvin and Hooper and Rowland Taylor and Bunyan and George Fox and Penn and Baxter and Flavel and Wesley and Zinzendorf and Francis Xavier and Eliot the Apostle of the Indians and Schwarz and Hans Egede and Howard and Neff and Henry Martyn, who by faith subdued kingdoms for Christ, wrought righteousness, obtained the fulfillment of the promises, stopped the mouths of blasphemers and filled them with hymns of praise, quenched the violence of hatred, melting it with love, out of weakness were made strong, waxed valiant in the fight against Satan and turned armies of aliens to bow before the name of the living God."

The sermon was preached before the University of Cambridge and one who was present reported that as the preacher summoned the mighty spirits from the past, there was breathless silence and a deep impression was made upon all present. History indeed can be made the handmaiden of faith. Nor must the preacher confine his study to the great figures of Christendom. The world drama in the pages of a Gibbon, a Ranke, a Creighton and even of an H. G. Wells is his inheritance. Let him claim it.

3. Biography

Thomas Arnold of Rugby advised writers and preachers to constantly make use of the biography of good men. A genuine biography enables us to see into the motives on which a man has built his life, the ideas with which he started, the enemies with whom he had to contend, the faith and the aspiration which gave him the victory. We see his strength and his weakness and we are stimulated to attempt great things. If he could do what he did, why may not we? Especially does the young minister in a remote country parish need the encouragement and stimulus to be derived from a knowledge of the lives of other preachers who under similar handicaps achieved great things. And the thoughts and comfort which he has found for himself he can communicate to others. How often is a dull sermon redeemed from futility by an incident taken

from the life-experience of a great man or woman,
an incident which has stirred the emotions or fired
the imagination of the preacher himself! There
are biographies which ought to be the familiar
friends of every minister of the Gospel, but of a
long list only a few need be named: — Stanley's
Life of Arnold, Prothero's *Life of Stanley*,
Brooke's *Life of Robertson*, Mrs. Kingsley's *Life
of Charles Kingsley*, Macleod's *Life of Norman
Macleod*, Maurice's *Life of F. D. Maurice*,
Allen's *Life of Phillips Brooks*, Abbott's *Life of
Beecher*, Barry's *Life of J. H. Newman*, Joseph
Parker's *Autobiography*, Povritt's *Life of J. H.
Jowett*, Major's *Life of Boyd Carpenter*, and
Robertson Nicoll's *Princes of the Church*. To be
made free of such high company is a spiritual
education, it is to put ourselves in the way of winning a wise bearing and a noble carriage in the
things of the soul. Who can read the lives of
these men without praying for greater consecration to the ideal and a more diligent use of all
his powers in the service of his fellows? Such
aspirations will turn the pulpit into a throne of
eloquence and of power.

4. Poetry

The message of the preacher is not only true,
it is beautiful and therefore, ought to be arrayed

in beautiful dress. And the only way in which we can gain a style at once suggestive and graceful is by a study of and feeling for the best poetry. It gives a rhythm and cadence — essentials in all good spoken discourse. Few men of science had such a command of vigorous and harmonious language as T. H. Huxley. He was nurtured on the Bible and Milton. John Bright read the poets for the enrichment of his style. Valuable as is the study of poetry as a means of enriching and beautifying the style of the preacher, its greatest value lies in its power to stimulate the imagination. The famous distinction by DeQuincey between " literature of knowledge " and " literature of power " is of vital significance for the man who would address his fellows on religion. Critical and historical knowledge is ever-changing. The passage of a few years puts it out of date. But the literature of power has within it the seed of immortality. The great poets and dramatists of the past never die — though we may smile at their astronomy and geography — and they evoke power in others. " Poetry is the interpretation of the universal element in human nature "; and that power by which the interpretation is made is the imagination.

A large part of the Bible is poetic in substance if not always in form. No man can steep his mind in the thought and expression of the unknown prophet of the exile without catching something of his grand style, his imaginative splendor. Coleridge and Bossuet studied the book of Isaiah, drawn to it because of its conceptions and the sublimity of its language. Poetry has power over us because it gives us a point of view different from and higher than the processes of the discursive understanding. It suggests; it stimulates mental and emotional attitudes towards truth; it takes us up to the mountain-tops whence we may behold in mystic vision the world as an ordered, beautiful whole. " Archimedes demanded only a fulcrum that with his lever he might lift the earth. This the speaker schooled in poetry, especially Hebrew poetry, possesses. He is above matter; he contemplates it in the vast sweep of his commanding gaze; he sways it with his slightest touch and raises it to heights undreamt of by minds confined to earth." The student and lover of poetry cannot present a one-sided doctrinaire sermon. As Niebergall remarks we can use epic, lyric and dramatic poetry not only to enliven single parts of a sermon but also as the basis for the construction of a sermon as a whole.

5. Fiction

When R. S. Storrs warns the preacher to avoid fiction or to read it only in the smallest degree he is betraying the prejudice of the old-fashioned puritanism in which he was trained. As a matter of fact fiction discharges a very important function in the lives of brain workers. Novels of the better kind teach us the secrets of the soul, give us an insight into the interlacing motives that determine human conduct. Moreover, noble and ennobling truths are seen not as pale abstractions or bloodless categories, but alive, full of dynamic force and illuminating power. Where can one see the sadness of sin or the transforming energy of the grace of penitence so vividly portrayed as in *The Scarlet Letter?* Do you wish to get a new insight into the mystery of atonement? Read Dostoieffsky's *Crime and Punishment.* Do you want to behold the transfiguring glory of forgiveness and pity? You have only to turn to Victor Hugo's *Les Misérables.* Do you seek a vision of human nature in its heights and depths, its nobility and sordidness, its shame and splendor, held fast in the grasp of terrible passions, emancipated and glorified by faith and love, in a word, the world, the flesh and the devil and their vanquisher, the solitary soul of man? Open your Balzac and the vision is yours. The novel like the drama holds up the mirror to nature and life, and the more the preacher knows of the soul as deep students of the soul have revealed it, the better will he be able to minister the truths of religion, the forgiving and regenerating grace of God in Jesus Christ.

But fiction can do something more for the busy parson. People who do things need the novel as a kind of mental medicine. They become fatigued both in nerves and mind; they need to be taken out of themselves, in a novel; they crave a psychic change even though their physical surroundings remain unaltered. I have been told that Sir Edward Grey, now Lord Grey of Falloden, in the early days of the War, when so much depended on him, read a detective story every night. The same thing was true of Kitchener. Mr. Basil King, the well-known novelist, told me that on one occasion he was the fourth man at a dinner of eight, the other three being James Bryce, Franklin MacVeagh, then Secretary of the Treasury, and Professor Pumpelly, the geologist. When the ladies went out and the men were left alone, these three distinguished persons did not fall to discussing the big topics of the hour. For a good thirty minutes they talked about *Queed*, a current novel of the day. They had all read it, all been interested in it, and debated on the love-theme like three schoolgirls. For the very reason that the subjects which filled their minds most of the time were so large they fell back for recreation on a piece of not too exacting fiction. Someone told Mr. King that he happened to be in a bookstore in Chicago when Theodore Roosevelt and his daughter Alice came in. Roosevelt was ordering half a dozen works and picked up Mr. King's book, *The Street Called Straight*, which was then on the market. " You won't like that, father," his daughter warned him. " All the people in it act like fools." " Let's have it, just the same," said the great Theodore, and took the book away with him. I may add that my old teacher, Dr. Fairbairn of Oxford, loved a good story and when wearied with the serious problems of theology, would lose himself in the romances of Walter Besant. The preacher needs, like other men, to unbend his bow, to get away from himself and his burdens, and to find refreshment in a new atmosphere where his whole mental horizon is put farther off. On the other hand, the reading of fiction when we need no such refreshment is weakening rather than strengthening. It is a safe rule never to read two novels in immediate succession. Serious and sustained mental effort involving some degree of exhaustion should be the only justification for passing through the gate of romance, apart from that kind of reading which is done for the purpose of making ourselves familiar with the great masterpieces of literature.

6. Science

Our age is nothing if not scientific. All our educational systems are becoming increasingly scientific. The worst thing you can say of an idea or a principle is, " It is unscientific." The preacher who refuses to make himself acquainted with the main results of modern scientific research cuts himself off from the currents of present-day thought, and while he may speak to generations dead and gone, he has no message for the people of his own day. As Frederick Denison Maurice said, that man will do the best work as a preacher who is interested in the questions which occupy the minds of his contemporaries. While it is true that the new thought of our time has profoundly disturbed the religious life of men and women, it is also true that it has had a purifying, expanding, and ennobling effect. For one thing there is no room in the modern pulpit for a parochial Deity. The discoveries of science, penetrating our everyday thinking, have immeasurably extended our notions of time and space. All around and about us and within us are infinitudes. A thousand stars, each one as great or greater than our own sun, blaze in the sky in a point of space so small that the naked eye can scarcely behold it. And what of man himself? The paltry allowance of mundane history allowed him by the theologians has vanished in the immense vistas of his scientific past, and these in turn seem small when contrasted with the unimaginable lapse of ages during which our earth has come to be. And matter itself disappears in supersensible realities. It is hardly too much to say that science has revolutionized our theologic thinking. Our doctrines of God, of salvation, of immortality, have cast off their pettiness, have taken on a grander aspect. Hence the preacher must steer clear of all obscurantism by a working knowledge of scientific principle and method. When the spirit of reform touches our theological seminaries they will make it impossible for any student to enter the ministry without a sound acquaintance with the general results of scientific research. When this is achieved we shall possess a clergy capable of retaining the respect of educated men, and without loss to their moral and spiritual fervor and their practical usefulness. Nor is it out of place to insist that even a general knowledge of the results of scientific research offers a rich mine of illustration for religious teachings. The works of God throw light upon the Word of God; or rather, all the great discoveries of man in art, science, and morality are so many words of God to him. The living Spirit is an ever revealing Spirit. " Let him that hath an ear hear what the Spirit *is saying* unto the churches." And especially let the young preacher listen for he stands on the threshold of a new world. Challenging voices summon him to prepare for the spiritual leadership of an age which believes in science as an indispensable instrument of civilization and progress but which has ceased to believe in it as an oracle competent to shed light on the unsolved riddles of morality and religion.

7. Sermon Literature

Many preachers decline to study the sermons of other men for fear that their own originality may suffer. As well might an artist-pupil refuse to frequent picture-galleries or study under trained guidance the works of the great masters! How can any art be learned if the learner declines to sit at the feet of men who have proved themselves masters of the art and whose creations are available for earnest and sympathetic study? Augustine, himself no mean preacher, argues that " as infants cannot learn to speak except by learning words and phrases from those who do speak, why should not men become eloquent without being taught any art of speech, but simply by reading and learning the speeches of eloquent men, and by imitating them as far as they can. . . . We know no one who is eloquent without having read and listened to the speeches and debates of eloquent men." [2] What Augustine here says of the

[2] *De Doct. Chr.* Bk. IV. Chap. IV.

expression of the sermon may with even greater truth and appropriateness be applied to its plan or structure, its pervading tone, and its dominating idea.

The analysis and comprehension of the more important sermons of such men as Robertson, Liddon, Newman, Martineau, Bushnell, Magee, Brooks, Parker, Dale, and J. H. Jowett, with a view to the discovery of their methods and aims in preaching, must bring to the student expansion of vision, and a firmer grasp of the technique of his art. Rightly used, these and other experts, so far from spoiling the student's originality, will stimulate it and will save it from the vagaries and brilliant shallowness which too often assume its garments. Liddon read a sermon every day for many years, and mastered the thought and method of Bossuet, Massillon and Schleiermacher. Brooks read and re-read Robertson, Bushnell, Martineau, Maurice and many another. Bishop Wilberforce was a keen critic of other preachers' sermons, and has left on record his judgments of their weak and strong points. J. H. Jowett studied carefully all his great English-speaking pulpit contemporaries in order to correct his one-sidedness in dealing with his themes. These men were among the freshest and the most stimulating preachers of their time.

The student of preaching would do well to

study sermons not primarily for their ideas but
in order to see how the masters of pulpit speech
treat their texts and subjects, how they plan their
discourses, what is their method of dividing and
illustrating them, and of driving their argument
home to the heart and conscience of the hearer.
Nor should he be content with the study of printed
sermons. He should take every opportunity to
hear all kinds of preachers, great and small, to
listen to them critically yet sympathetically. Is
he deeply impressed, moved to think and to do
better things? He should ask himself, why?
Does the sermon leave him cold and unrespon-
sive? Again, he should question himself as to
the reason. He should compare his own style and
method of putting things with those of some
preacher whose sermon has delighted him and
persuaded him. There is no better discipline for
the preacher than to occupy the pew betimes and to
judge the pulpit from the standpoint of the hearer.
Even the wandering evangelist should not be
neglected. To dismiss him as a fanatic or an emo-
tionalist is easy but it is also foolish and ignorant.
A distinguished University teacher heard Gipsy
Smith once, and on coming away a friend criti-
cized the sermon and asked the professor's opinion. The professor replied that doubtless the
critic was right but that he (the professor) was at
that particular moment thinking more of his own

sins than of the preacher's homiletics. No man can address with power immense audiences night after night on the great questions of religion who has not within him a living spring of virtue, however poor a scholar, philosopher or theologian he may be. Still less can such a man make others feel the reality of the world to come if the powers of that other world have not touched his own soul. Professional or academic pride does but condemn itself when it shrinks from learning the lessons such men can teach.

III

PREPARATION FOR PREACHING

II. Special Preparation

Here let us assume that the work of preparing to compose a sermon for the following Sunday, is now to be entered upon. What is the first step? I answer: *to begin early in the week*. Real sermons are growths not manufactured articles. The man who never thinks of his discourse till Friday night or Saturday morning and then betakes himself to some ready-made sketches from a volume of outlines and a dictionary of illustrations, may produce something which will tide him over the Sunday but he is making impossible the attainment of pulpit competence, not to speak of the serious moral injury he is inflicting upon his own nature. It is no excuse to say that there is no time in the life of a busy clergyman to brood over his discourse throughout the week. Kingsley's life was crowded with all sorts of duties, yet he chose his subject on the preceding Sunday evening and talked it over with his wife, took a good rest on Monday, but on Tuesday he sketched an outline of the sermon. Then it was put aside for a couple of days and on Friday it was finished. Brooks chose his theme on Monday, took time to gather his materials and to allow the theme gradually to take possession of him and on Wednesday began to write the sermon, finishing it by Friday. J. H. Jowett also began his preparations for Sunday's sermons on Tuesday, and spent two days in thinking out and writing each sermon. Not until the time came, says his biographer, when the central idea of his sermon could be crystallized into one short luminous sentence was a theme ripe enough for Jowett to begin serious work upon it in the study. He confessed that getting that germinal sentence was the most exacting and one of the most essential elements in sermon preparation. The truth is that clergymen will find plenty of time to do what they ought to do as soon as they imitate other professional men whose duties compel them to systematize their time, and to cultivate the grace of punctuality. There is, perhaps, no body of men so guilty of frittering away their time in trivialities, in a fussy parade of being busy as ministers of religion. They need the Apostolic admonition to be written over their desks, " Study to be quiet and to mind your own business," especially the business of preaching. It is to be feared that the task of sitting down and grappling with a text or a sub-

ject whether in the mood for it or not has less
attractions than " dropping in " at a kindly parishioner's house to have a talk about the Boy Scouts
or the Girls' Friendly or a parish meeting to be
held sometime in the coming week. Everything
that is not really vital should be vigorously ex-
cluded to make room for the work of those thirty
minutes in which, as Ruskin says, you have to raise
the dead.

You have now determined to begin the sermon
in good season. Where shall you find your subject or text? The best sermons are those which
grow out of a great text or theme that has seized
your mind and will not let it go until you have
uttered its message. Sometimes the subject is suggested by one's general reading, or by a chance remark made in the course of a serious conversation
with a friend or by a contemporary happening in
the political or religious world, or by a text which
shines in a new and fascinating light. Dr. James
Black, the Edinburgh preacher, rightly advises
that a book should be kept in which texts with the
train of thought suggested by them should be entered. "This saves you from the week-end
tragedy of hunting for subjects, a dreary and
soul-scarifying performance. And still further,
this offers you a subject on which you already
have a line like a fish on a hook." [1] The next

---

[1] *The Mystery of Preaching*, p. 79.

step is to find a suitable text with which the subject may be connected. But here let the preacher beware! For the pulpit is too often disgraced by the forced adaptation of the text to the needs of the sermon, with the resultant imposition of false meanings on the words of the Scripture writers.

If you are a serious and critical student of the Bible, you will have little difficulty in finding a text to suit your theme. But if by chance the right text should not suggest itself, omit the text and proceed with your discourse. The text may be connected with the subject as the statement of a general principle is related to a particular instance. For example, if you wish to point out the harm resulting from a too literal interpretation of some commonly accepted article of religious belief, you can do so while speaking from the text: " The letter killeth but the spirit giveth life." You can use such a text deductively reasoning from the general idea to the particular instance. Or you may connect the text and the subject inductively, and argue from a particular instance to a general principle. Thus, take the study of St. Peter's vision of the sheet let down from Heaven. When told to " kill and eat," he replied, " Not so, Lord, for I have never eaten anything that is common or unclean." The immediate subject was the barrier between Jew and Gentile, but from this can be drawn various applications of the general lesson that a tradition which has never been challenged is injurious to the progress of truth and the life of the spirit.

Or you may, begin with a text — and this is the preferable method for the novice — and let the subject develop out of it. But why select a text at all? Why indeed? There is no moral or intellectual obligation. And many a man has taken a text and then proceeded with a sermon quite remote from the sense of Scripture. George Wharton Pepper protests against the use of a text at the beginning of the sermon but his opposition is only as to the place of the text *not* as to the text itself. There are solid advantages in the use of a Scriptural passage which may not be dispensed with except for sound and unusual reasons. One is that you awaken the curiosity of the hearer. Another is that it lends to the main idea of your sermon the spiritual authority of the Bible. And still another is that, if rightly chosen, it will serve the interests of unity and progress. Moreover, why should we shock the conventions unless we are sure that a gain commensurate with the disturbance will result?

If you begin by choosing a text, treat it with respect. There is an old-fashioned rule not yet abrogated, "All sound preaching rests on sound exegesis." The text must not be torn from its context but it must be illumined by it. Do not, for example, fall into T. H. Huxley's blunder when he attributed to St. Paul the argument: " If the dead are not raised, let us eat and drink for tomorrow we die." The Apostle is pointing out the inference which the vast majority of men would draw from a denial of immortality, — an inference which he believes makes the denial morally reprehensible. He was far too inward and ethical in his thinking to make the moral life dependent on belief in a future existence. A distinguished minister preached once in one of our American pulpits from a highly poetic text the original meaning of which he neglected to look up. His argument was sound and his thoughts worthy of the occasion, but they rested on the wrong foundations. It happened that a scholar-journalist was present in the congregation and he took occasion to hold up the preacher to scorn for his failure to do justice to the prophetic word. A warning against slovenly and incompetent handling of the truth!

What sort of text should be chosen? The popular notion that anything within the covers of the Bible is capable of being made the basis of a sermon is, of course, absurd. There is much that does not lend itself to sermonic treatment, though the preacher may use it for illustrative purposes. As a rule it is wise to select texts which set forth some great truth in striking or imaginative language. Study the texts of the great masters and you will find that they are almost always splendid, suggestive, illuminating. " There is a nibbling way of treating the sacred book," says J. O. Dykes, " which snips off from it little tags, bits that may no doubt suggest or infer much more than they say, but which by themselves say very little. It is better surely to take a portion which, whatever its length, has within it bulk and depth of meaning adequate to fill the sermon and to feed the flock." [2] Do you say that great texts require a knowledge and skill such as preachers at the beginning of their career cannot be entrusted to possess? I answer: far better to achieve a splendid failure than a mean success. It is by the effort to grapple with big themes that the preacher grows in spiritual strength and compass. I would also plead for the use of unhackneyed texts. They stimulate the preacher's powers of originality, and impart freshness and unexpectedness to his message. The hearer's attention is caught at once and his curiosity is awakened. " A novel text is a new voice." Here is an example of how a text of this sort can be made to yield valuable lessons in the spiritual life. The preacher is the well-known English Congregationalist, Dr. J. D. Jones of Bournemouth.[3] His text is II Chron. XVIII,

[2] *The Christian Minister and His Duties*, pp. 233, 234.
[3] *The Hope of the Gospel*, pp. 55–68.

33: " A certain man drew a bow at a venture and smote the King of Israel between the joints of the harness." After explaining about the war between Ahab and the King of Syria and pointing out that the forces of the Syrian King were ordered to concentrate their attack on the King of Israel, the preacher proceeds: " So what you have is this, you have a whole army out for the purpose of killing one bad man. . . . Spite of all their efforts Ahab remained unhurt. And then some unknown soldier drew a bow at a venture. That random shot smote the King of Israel." The story illustrates a law in the spiritual world. There are things which can be got by not seeking them diligently. (1) *Happiness*. You cannot get it by making it your aim. Seek to do your duty, to serve others. You get happiness by not seeking it, by seeking something quite different. (2) *Honor*. The respect and regard of your fellows cannot be got by aiming at them directly. The man who plans schemes for honor never gets it, but he who spends himself in the service of others, sooner or later wins the high respect and admiration of his fellows. The lives of David Livingstone and William Booth illustrate this principle. (3) *Life*. To save life is to lose it; " we get life, full broad, and abundant life, not by seeking it and saving it but by ' giving it away.' " (4) *Goodness*. Even a noble character is attained not by discreetly aiming at it but by loving Christ. "Love the appeal of Christ and when men love Christ goodness follows and becomes easy. Thus from an old story which in itself has but a passing interest, and a text which does not at first sight seem to promise much, the genius of the preacher builds up an admirable discourse, full of life, color and movement. Let me mention a few other texts which, at first sight, do not seem to offer much but from which good sermons have been preached, and from which good sermons can be preached again: Exodus XXXIV, 29, "And Moses wist not that the skin of his face shone." John XX, 8, "Then entered in therefrom that other disciple." Exodus XXVII, 24, "So they gave it me; then I cast it into the fire and there came out this calf." Esther IV, 2, "And he came even before the King's gate; for none might enter within the King's gate clothed with sackcloth." II Samuel XVI, 11, "And David said, let him curse; for the Lord hath bidden him." "The mirage shall become a pool." [4] Isaiah XXX, 7.

Having chosen the text or the subject, what is the next step? Here experts differ. Some advise that the preacher should set about the work of collecting materials, others suggest that he should

[4] The preachers on the above cited texts in order are: Elmslie, Bushnell, Brooks, Watkinson, Denney, J. H. Jowett.

think out his subject in general outline, and depend, in the main, on his acquired knowledge and experience for the working out of his ideas. Both methods are good — each will choose what best suits his mental aptitudes. There are many who must light their fires at another's flame. To have a general conception of what we wish to discuss or expound is advisable to start with. This central idea will gather round it thoughts, illustrations, memories, flashes of poetic imagery. As I have elsewhere said, the subconscious mind will get to work and when the time for writing arrives, you will have the nucleus of your discourse at hand.

The first business to set about consciously is to understand the text, if its meaning is not upon the surface. Consult for this purpose the most competent exegetes, and do not tie yourself to the pronouncements of any one of them. As a rule English Biblical scholars are strong in criticism and exegesis, but weak in theology, while the reverse holds true of Scottish divines; they are weak on the exegetical but strong on the theological side. Read the text in Moffatt's and Goodspeed's translations as well as in the Revised Version, and if possible in at least one foreign rendering. This process by itself will yield valuable suggestions. Search out parallel passages and note whatever fresh light they may throw upon the text. Look steadily at the text with your own eyes, and ask yourself: What does it say *to me?* Then examine your card-index for reference to relevant literature or consult your note-book for any quotations or impressions listed under appropriate headings. Your materials are now before you. Do a little hard thinking at this stage until the plan of your sermon gradually takes shape. The question is often asked: Is it advisable to read another man's sermon on a text from which you are going to preach? I remember John Watson saying that once before writing his sermon on a certain occasion he took pains to read Robertson's sermon on the same text. He found in completing the discourse that it was Robertson — only weaker; and the manuscript had to descend into the waste-paper basket. On the whole a young preacher will be well advised to work out with the aid of such materials as he has assembled his own main line of thought. Only after he has preached his sermon should he read what another preacher has to say on the same theme. In building up his discourse he need not fear the charge of plagiarism if he takes care to assimilate and to re-create mentally the material he has borrowed. Do not aim at originality, the besetting weakness of the ambitious. Newman has said somewhere that there are some things which can be got only by renouncing them. Originality is one of them. Renounce it and instead aim at veracity of thought, reality of feeling and exactness of expression, and your individuality will make for itself abundant channels of communication. The very way in which you use your materials should be carefully watched. For example, what is to be done in the matter of quotations and illustrations?

1. *Quotations.* Be on your guard against overquotation. Some sermons give the impression that the preacher has emptied upon his manuscript large portions of his commonplace book. I once heard a sermon in which there must have been fifteen quotations from authors ancient and modern, and such a patchwork of scattered thoughts from all regions of the intellectual world does that discourse appear to me now that I am astonished at my own moderation in reckoning the august total!

Such lavishness in the use of other men's opinions betrays an imperfect confidence in our own. It also indicates failure to master thoroughly the material of the sermon. Moreover, the constant citation of passages from this, that, or the other " eminent divine " or " great philosopher " distracts the attention of the hearer from the main drift of the sermon, especially if, as is frequently the case, such passages stand out by virtue of some unusual felicity of expression, putting to shame the less striking literary creations of the preacher's own. And yet the use of quotations is not to be put wholly under the ban. I observe that Dean Inge, the Bishop of Durham (Dr. Henson), and Dr. R. J. Campbell among English preachers, Dr. Fosdick and Dr. George Gordon among American pulpit speakers, like to quote but they rarely transgress the limits of good taste. Their method is worthy of study. There is no part of the sermon structure which requires greater care and tact than that of quotation, and only practice can prevent unhappy mistakes. Dr. James Black in his *Mystery of Preaching* quotes the late Professor Denney against quotation but fails to note that scarcely one of the professor's published sermons is without a number of quotations, some of them of considerable bulk! Brevity, importance, relevance, and freshness; surely any quotations which can emerge unscathed from all these acid tests may be allowed a place in the sermon.

2. *Illustrations.* There are sound pedagogic reasons for a liberal yet not quixotically liberal use of illustrations. The congregation has certain claims upon the preacher, and one is that he shall be intelligible, and intelligibility depends on clearness of thought. An illustration has as one of its functions to make clear whatever threatens to be obscure. It ought, however, to do more than act as a window to let in light. When discussion and exhortation fail to kindle the imagina-

tion or to touch the emotions, an apt illustration will succeed in doing both. "We illustrate in order to make real." Both functions of illustration, illumination and realization are exemplified in Alexander Maclaren's use of a familiar object as a symbol of the spiritual life: ".You and I write our lives as if on one of those manifold writers which you use. A thin filmy sheet *here*, a bit of black paper below it; but the writing goes through upon the next page; and when the blackness which divides two worlds is swept away *there* the history of each life written by ourselves remains legible in eternity." Such an illustration sticks in the mind, and the truth it figures is recalled every time we see a manifold writer in use. There are persons who seem to have a gift of analogical visions. Wherever they go, they see everything as symbolical of something beyond itself. It is a high quality of mind that

" Finds tongues in trees, books in the running brooks,
  Sermons in stones "

but it is by no means common. Some preachers mournfully confess that the power to conceive an illustration seems to them impossible; they are at home in the abstract but far from home in the concrete. Yet without some measure of illustrative quality the sermonic style must prove flat, uninteresting, and stagnant. One can see how an audience " sits up and takes notice " (as the vulgar phrase goes) the moment the preacher forsakes his didactic manner and begins with: " Only yesterday I saw in the newspaper the story of a noble act of heroism performed by an unknown stranger." There is great encouragement in the fact that some of the most brilliant masters of illustration in the modern pulpit, notably Beecher, won these gifts by hard work, observation, and practice.

How then, you will ask, am I to gain the faculty of illustration? Not, I think, by recourse to books provided for that purpose. For the mechanical transference of an illustration from a book to your sermon cannot help your mind to create, it can only serve to make it less capable of finding those analogies between the spiritual and the material which serve to give point and clearness to your speech. By far the best illustrations are those which have come to you in your experience. And experience includes everything that has entered vitally into your life. Your reading, whether it be a biography, or a scientific primer, or a newspaper or a poem, or a novel, or the history of a country, will offer you a significant saying or a dramatic incident which, if you keep the mind alert, will link itself up with a thought that you purpose to develop in a sermon. Of course unless you have a Macaulay-like memory, you will make a note of the passage under a suitable heading in your " sermon seed-book."

Valuable as these excerpts may be they are secondary in effectiveness and interest to an experience of your own, a conversation with a friend, a sight in a country road, a memory of foreign travel, an impression made by a play which you have witnessed, the tragedy of some life failure known to you, the glory, of temptation overcome and sin trampled under foot shining in a heart whose confidence you have shared. These illustrations have a peculiar power; they cannot be doubted as you are yourself guarantee of their truthfulness, whereas, it is to be feared, many anecdotes culled from unaccredited sources are told in the pulpit which would hardly bear the strain of critical analysis. There is another source from which we may, draw freely and to which many preachers do not have recourse, with loss to themselves and their hearers.

The Bible is crowded with stories, incidents, situations, similes, metaphors, parables, symbolisms, analogies between things material and things spiritual. Such preachers as Robertson and Liddon have known how to use these materials to make clear the truths or to intensify its power over the imagination and the heart. They have set us a good example, and if we follow it we may succeed in inducing the average churchgoer to read his

Bible.   A warning word may not be out of place. Don't illustrate what needs no illustrating.   I once asked the late Austin Smith whether he liked a sermon which he had just heard a distinguished preacher deliver.   " I would have liked it," he replied, " if Dr. . . . had not insisted on piling upon me a mass of illustrations in support of a truth which it never occurred to me or any other Christian to doubt."

IV

THE STRUCTURE OF THE SERMON

ONE of the most common faults in preaching is want of coherence, lack of plan. A sermon may contain good ideas, interesting illustrations, and elevated language, yet leave no impression on the hearer's mind, simply because it has followed no principle of construction. One may say that order, which is Heaven's first law, is also the first law of the sermon. Hence the imperative need of a plan, a definite arrangement of the material which you have assimilated. A study of the great preachers will show that without exception their discourses were built up in accordance with a carefully thought out scheme of arrangement. Every man will choose the method that best suits his mental quality, but method of some kind there must be. And it must not be the method of the lecture or the essay. To impose upon the sermon the character of either of these literary forms is to dig the sermon's grave. The religious discourse has a special aim, deals with a particular class of subjects, is given as part of a particular function and

to a specific type of audience. It has its own
rules and principles which have been tested by
centuries of practice. No one can with impunity
violate the underlying structural principles of this
particular form of literary product. The words
of Vinet on this matter are weighty and deserve to
be pondered by every student of the preaching
art. " Oratorical discourse, and especially that of
the pulpit has a double purpose: to instruct and to
persuade. . . . We are instructed only in so far
as we comprehend and retain; but we comprehend
and retain easily, surely, only in the proportion
in which the matters on which our understanding
is exercised are consecutive and connected. Teaching in which order is wanting, hardly deserves
the name of teaching; all that it can do is to give
more or less valuable information. The incon-
venience of the order in this respect is not merely
negative; if it is unhappy not to be understood,
it is more unhappy to be misunderstood. The bad
arrangement of the sermon exposes our hearers to
this danger. . . . It is impossible that it should
be otherwise. *A badly ordered discourse is obscure and that which is obscure is weak.* A discourse in which the main laws of order are violated is contrary to the nature of the human mind,
to its just expectation, to its wants." [1]   Vinet in
this connection quotes Quintilian, the greatest

[1] *Homiletics or the Theory of Preaching*, pp. 265, 266.

teacher of public speech in the ancient world: " A speech wanting the quality of order, wanders about like a ship without a steersman, incoherent with itself, full of repetitions and omissions, losing its way as by night, in unknown paths."

It is obvious that an oral address on religious truths with a view to instruct and persuade must have a subject which needs to be introduced to the attention of the hearer, to be developed, to be directed to heart and conscience and to be urged upon his will. Hence the general scheme, within which there may be and ought to be great variety, is given in the nature of the sermon itself. That sermon will be weak and fruitless which is without cohesion, the parts of which are not organically related to each other and to the controlling idea. Be it noted that the demand for order is not satisfied when you have arranged your material after the traditional scheme of Introduction, Development, and Conclusion. It is in the body of the discourse that this law must especially rule. Here is really where the secret of strength lies. It may be compared to the vertebral column that sustains the organism. To be weak here is to be weak everywhere.

Hence the preacher should not be content with the first arrangement that comes to mind. He should turn the matter over and over again and do some hard thinking until he has assured himself that he has obtained the order which will best achieve his purpose. To spend more time and thought on this part of the mechanism of the discourse than on any other will bring its own reward in an increased mastery of your material, in a sense of cumulative power, and in the quality of intellectual impressiveness. But the order need not always be obvious. Occasionally at least the plan of the sermon might be so made as to resemble the well-constructed plot of a great novel. The action begins to turn around. The sermon culminates when it has completed the circle. The hearer is kept wondering and alert, asks himself — What is he going to make of this? What is to be the outcome? His interest is seized, his mind is compelled to work, and he is drawn along irresistibly to the inevitable end. Comment is needless, exhortation unnecessary, the significance of the whole now bursts upon him, and conviction coincides with the conclusion.

Let us now consider the formal elements in the structure of the sermon.

1. The Introduction

Frequently we can take a short and easy way with the introduction. Dismiss it and pass at once to the development of your subject. Why explain if there is nothing to be explained? Why seek to conciliate your audience as the ancient orators did when your audience is already friendly and awaits your deliverance? Why spend time in making an introduction disconnected with the main theme in order to gain the attention, as some writers of rhetoric recommend, when you can win the interest of your hearers in simpler and less devious ways?

Certainly there is nothing more likely to *slay* interest at the outset than the long, dreary, conventional statements, now historical, now geographical, into which some preachers lead up to their subjects. The young preacher must, from the beginning, learn that, as Dr. Phelps remarks, the first few minutes should lay down a magnetic line between the pulpit and the pew which shall vibrate with electric response all the way through. This is the vital thing to remember whether there is anything in the nature of an introduction or not. What has been said of a wig is equally pertinent to a sermon. " It is perfect with a head, perfect without a head; perfect with a tail, perfect without a tail; perfect with either, neither or both."

Still, more often than not, an introduction of some sort is necessary. Whatever parts of the sermon may be left unwritten the opening sentences, which should be short, crisp, and suggestive, ought to be carefully thought out and put down on paper. Begin quietly. As a preacher of a former generation used to say: "Begin slow; speak low; catch fire; rise higher." Avoid an opening on a high key whether of voice or thought. Beware of

> "Vaulting ambition, which o'erleaps itself
> And falls on t'other."

The main function of the introduction is to arouse what the psychologists call "expectant attention." An excellent illustration is to be found in a sermon by Phillips Brooks in Westminster Abbey. "This is a wonderful age in which we live. So men are constantly in the habit of saying to each other. So, no doubt, men have always said about their ages. There can hardly ever have been a time which, to the men who lived in it, did not seem full of emphatic and remarkable differences which distinguished it from all other times, and made it very wonderful and strange. . . . It is a wonderful age not merely in the number of strange unprecedented things which are happening in it, the strange unprecedented character that belongs to it as a whole, but also in the prominence of wonder as an element in the view which it takes of itself. It is a wonderful age because it is an age full of wonder."

Or note how Stopford Brooke introduces his sermon on "Days of Judgment." "Whether we believe in God or not it is plain that there are days of judgment, when nations and men are sifted, wheat from chaff, folly from wisdom, weakness from strength; days in which the warning is given or punishment exacted, destruction administered or salvation gained. At any rate there is an order in the affairs of men."

Of what should the introduction consist? First of all: nothing should be put into it which belongs to some other part of the sermon. It should introduce but not discuss. Then, if possible, a point of contact should be found with some event of contemporary history or with an experience of the preacher, or with a book or article that has stirred the public mind. Perhaps all that is necessary may be simply a brief explanation of the terms of the text, or a hurried sketch of the historical background of the passage selected for discussion. Avoid a stereotyped mode of introducing your sermons. Aim at variety. Let the first sentence be sometimes an exclamation of surprise, or a rhetorical question, or an historical allusion, or a Biblical scene known to your hearers. Whatever form the opening sentences may take they should be pertinent to the subject and lead straight to it.

2. The Statement of the Theme

Custom varies as to the precise point in the sermon when the theme should be stated. Some preachers announce it at once and then proceed with the introduction. This was the favorite method of C. C. Hall, former President of the Union Theological Seminary. Others hold in reserve the theme until near the end; but only a very practiced orator can do this with success. It would seem that the psychological place is at the close of the preacher's introductory remarks. So important did Cardinal Newman esteem the statement of his theme to be that he recommended the preacher to place a distinct categorical proposition before him such as he could write down in a form of words, and then to guide his preparation by it and to aim at bringing out its meaning and nothing else. Newman said that his own aim in all his preaching and writing was to make his thoughts and expressions as definite as possible. Definiteness in his view, was the prime virtue of a sermon. This idea fits in, of course, with Roman Catholic dogmatic and disciplinary ideals, but is out of harmony with modern feeling and temper of mind. Today what men ask for in a sermon is not so much definiteness as suggestiveness; they long for the far as well as the near horizons. If the introduction is properly conceived and expressed it will of itself help the intelligent hearer to understand what the theme or fundamental thought of the sermon is to be. Unhappily there are in every congregation persons who are not intelligent or at least not intelligent when they cross the threshold of a church, and we must help them. And this is best done by a clear, sententious, simple sentence indicating what you propose to do.

A few illustrations of how eminent preachers state their themes may be useful.

The well-known London preacher, Dr. R. F. Horton begins a sermon thus: " The subject tonight is ' The Price of Sin.' Fools make a mock of sin, philosophers sometimes explain it away, and theologians often, in their discussions, manage to transfer it from the region of the conscience into that of the intellect. But it always remains a stern and inexorable fact. . . . Now my object tonight is to show how Jesus Christ, our Lord, paid the price of sin, how he was the propitiation for our sins, and not for ours only but for those of the whole world; and how it is that not only preëminently but essentially and absolutely, it makes him the Saviour of the world." Or take this from a striking sermon on " Temptation " by George Adam Smith. After giving out as his text Matthew IV, 1. " Then was Jesus led up of the Spirit into the wilderness to be tempted of the Devil " he announces his theme thus: " I do not intend to go into the details of the three forms of temptation recorded in this chapter. Let us abide by the first verse of the story and consider the general elements of temptation which that describes." He then proceeds to map out his discourse.

Observe the simple yet effective way in which Dr. W. Russell Bowie introduces and announces his theme. Taking for his text Psalm XXXVI, 9, " In Thy light shall we see light," he finds his point of contact at once in a fragment from the published letters of Franklin K. Lane, penned on the day before his death: " It would lend such impulse to see clearly." That is what people in bereavement or in mental perplexity need above everything. Light. When we use that word we take up into our intellectual and spiritual meanings the metaphors of our physical senses. The truth and understanding which we want must have for us the values which light has as set in contrast with darkness. Let us think then, at the beginning, specifically of what those values are." [2] The preacher, then, proceeds to set forth some of the values of physical light, and he finds these to be symbolic of the light of God in Jesus Christ. The central thought expressed in the theme announced is never let go but is developed in masterly fashion throughout.

Dr. J. Fort Newton in a sermon on " The Life After Death," after an impressive introduction on the mystery of death, asks the question: " Must

[2] See *Best Sermons, 1924* (pp. 3–26).

we then admit that we know nothing about the life after death, and are doomed to live in a world of dim hints and cryptic analogies with no glad, triumphant assurance?   Far, very far from it! Indeed the whole point of my sermon is to show that we know much — very much — about the life after death both as to its reality and its conditions — all, in fact, that we really need to know — and if we are wise enough to lay the facts to heart, we shall find consolation for today and inspiration for the morrow." [3]

Whatever may be our way of informing the congregation of what our purpose is in addressing them, it is clear that the purpose itself should not only be in the centre of our minds but in the centre of their minds as well.

There are certain rules which beginners in the art of preaching will do well to observe. (1) Where the words of a text are clear and perfectly intelligible, you have your theme ready for use.   To translate the terms of the text into other words would be to spoil them.   An excellent illustration is given by Archdeacon Charles, who, taking for his text, "In your patience you shall win your souls," states his theme as "The Winning of the Soul."   (2) The theme should not contain any technical terms or any word employed in an unusual sense.   Robertson, preaching from

[3] *Great Modern Sermons* (pp. 167–178).

John VII, 17, " If any man will do his will, he shall know of the doctrine whether it be of God," phrases his subject as " Obedience the organ of spiritual knowledge." Here the word " organ " is a philosophical term, meaning the instrument or agent by which we gain knowledge. Obedience is not the organ of knowledge in this sense. John Watson preaching from the same text silently corrects Robertson and gives as his theme: " Practical obedience the condition of spiritual knowledge." (3) The theme should contain in clearest wording what you propose to develop in the discourse. Fenelon's oft-quoted remark is to the point: " the discourse is the theme developed and the theme is the discourse summarized." Avoid all vague and hazy phrases. On the other hand, be careful not to alienate your hearers by a tone offensively dogmatic or after the manner of the typical schoolmaster. (4) The theme should be specifically formulated. Vast subjects such as " Divine Providence," " Faith," " God," should be limited to certain aspects or angles, otherwise there is danger that a sermon clouded with vague generalities will be the outcome. Nearly all the great preachers take for the subject of one or more sermons, " Immortality," but when the sermons are studied it will be found that the problem is narrowed to one or two points of view, as for example, the " desire of immortality," or " the power of immortality," or "immortality and the resurrection of Christ." This is as it should be. (5) The theme should express one topic for discussion. It is a serious fault to deal with a number of diverse subjects. The mind of the hearer is confused when the preacher jumps from one idea to another, without working out any one of them to a satisfactory conclusion. This does not mean that a sermon should contain only one idea, as Archbishop Magee, Chalmers and J. H. Jowett maintained, but that unity of impression should be maintained by seeing to it that the ideas have an organic relation to each other. To follow Magee's advice " never to have more than one idea and to arrange every sentence with a view to that," is to impose upon the pulpit an intolerable limitation.

3. The Development of the Theme

It is helpful to draw up an outline of the plan as you gather the materials, and it may be that when the materials are all assembled you will have to modify the plan. Robertson describes his method of sermon composition thus: " I first make copious notes; then draw out a form (rough plan); afterwards write copiously, sometimes twice or thrice the thoughts, to disentangle them into a connected whole; then make a syllabus, and lastly a skeleton which I take into the pulpit."

Be master of your plan and change it while composing the sermon, if your thought demands a change.

The structure of the sermon demands clearly marked stages of thought which go by the name of divisions. Young preachers are prone to revolt against the use of divisions. They feel that the practice is injurious to spontaneity and freedom and gives the sermon a hard, scholastic look. Doubtless also a desire to break away from the conventions of the pulpit has something to do with this dislike of what seems " old-fashioned " and " out of date." The common-sense advice of Dr. Johnson is confirmed by modern experts in teaching and preaching: " The divisions not only help the memory of the hearer but direct the judgment of the writer; they supply sources of invention and keep every part in its proper place." [4] We may add that a scheme of division prevents vagueness and indefiniteness of treatment. Too often the preacher enters upon a second argument before he has finished the first, and then finishes the first when he ought to be busy with the second. To the argument that the hearer is liable to grow weary of a sermon with divisions, it may be replied that he would grow still more weary of a sermon without them. Nor if skilfully used do they really break the con-

[4] Boswell's *Life of Johnson*, vol. III, p. 506 (Hill's ed.).

tinuity of the discourse. It is over-division or failure to link the end of one division with the beginning of the next, or the linking of them in a mechanical way, that gives the sermon an aspect of fragments of thought flung together, like a heap of stones. But after all, the divisions of a sermon have nothing sacrosanct about them. They make simple the means by which the promise of the sermon given in the theme, is accomplished. If a better method can be devised let the preacher by all means use it. Only let him see to it that the sermon can bear analysis; if it cannot, his method is a failure.

Granted that divisions are helpful and to be employed, should the congregation be informed of them beforehand? This used to be the almost invariable custom of the pulpit. Massillon, for example, does not try to conceal his complicated divisions and sub-divisions and sub-sub-divisions, but flaunts them in the face of the congregation. The Puritans agreed with the great French Catholic preacher at least in this matter. Their sermons appear to us dreary and artificial because of their form, though they made a great impression in their own time. The present fashion is against announcing the divisions as too formal and savoring somewhat of pedantry. But some successful preachers call in question the wisdom of this criticism. Dr. J. Paterson-Smyth writes:

" When I began preaching I used not to announce the heads or divisions of my sermon. It seemed to me stiff and formal and old-fashioned. And, of course, like all young preachers, I must be original. I have changed my mind about that, as about many other things. I do not formally announce my divisions, but I take great pains to let the audience know them. You must remember that a preached sermon is not like a printed one, where the reader can see the divisions and paragraphs and where he can look back to the beginning of a passage for the connection. If the congregation are not helped in some way to guess at the coming line of thought, they get confused very soon, and you lose their attention." [5] In this matter claim for yourself freedom and refuse to be bound by the words of any master. If the sermon is highly argumentative and logical, an audience of the average kind will follow your discourse better, if they know at the outset how you propose to handle your theme. In that case you will do well to announce your divisions in words that are clear, terse and easily remembered. But in the ordinary course of preaching, and certainly when dealing with subjects rather than texts, it is advisable to let the sermon develop point by point, and at the close to gather up in pregnant, well-turned sentences the thoughts you have expounded.

[5] *The Preacher and His Sermon*, p. 136.

The stages of thought in a sermon are subject to certain rules. But within limits, considerable freedom will best serve the ends of preaching. One rule often violated especially by young preachers is that due attention should be paid to *all* the divisions. Over-dwelling on one division lessens the interest of the hearer and destroys the symmetry of the discourse. The sermon must not gyrate around one point, it must move onward, and when you have sufficiently impressed one point on the minds of the audience, pass on at once to the next. Vinet rightly says that the oratorical disposition of a sermon is as necessary as the logical. The logical satisfies the mind but the oratorical is necessary to touch the emotions and move the will. Now the oratorical movement means that the discourse is a continued movement of ideas, carrying the hearer onward to a conclusion felt to be inevitable. Then again, the sense of progress which characterizes a good sermon implies a definite order determined by the quality and importance of the elements of the discussion. The weaker arguments must precede the stronger, tranquil assertions before moving appeals, a quiet argument before an earnest exhortation. Subtleties, over-refinement, confusion of material belonging to one division with that belonging to another are faults which go far to nullify the purpose intended to be served by divisions.

Of vital importance is the right method of

passing from one division to the next. No part of the preacher's work requires greater skill and delicacy than this. The advice of Boyd Carpenter here is valuable. "The way to avoid hesitancy and clumsiness is to make a collection of what I call 'bridge-words' — sets of phrases to be used in such transitions. Have a number of these always at command and you will have no difficulty about it." [6] It is the practice of these precepts which give the sermon the quality of naturalness and spontaneity — the secret of aesthetic satisfaction, as well as of direct access to the emotions and the will.

4. The Conclusion

"It is an established law of oratory that the orator shall have a definite and positive conclusion; the sermon is under the same regulation. . . . At this point weakness is unpardonable." [7] It is generally agreed that the two parts of the sermon most easily ruined are the introduction and the conclusion. Some preachers end without completing their thought; others finish what they have to say and then, by a fatal aberration, go on to add a conclusion. In both cases the hearer goes away discontented and unhappy. We must recall that

[6] *Life and Letters*, p. 118.
[7] Davis: *Principles of Preaching*, p. 217.

the sermon is a work of art and this is bad artistry. For the conclusion is the crown and culmination of your work throughout the sermon. To go wrong here is to fail in accomplishing the purpose for which you entered the pulpit, the capture of the will in order that the truth expounded may be realized in change of thought and life.

Some may object that the application should be diffused throughout the sermon, and that, therefore, anything in the nature of a formal conclusion will be rendered unnecessary. It is true that for sermons of a textual character this objection holds good, only, however, to a certain extent. Even when warmth and practical reference have pervaded the body of the discourse, it may be appropriate on occasion for the preacher to make a more direct and definite application at the end. When a subject rather than a text has been dealt with, a conclusion is a necessity. As an aid to memory the hearer needs to have brought before him briefly and skilfully as a whole the various ideas and motives which have already been presented one by one.

As a rule the sermon should end on a personal note. A great jurist once said that when he went to hear the Gospel preached he wished to have it made a *personal* matter, and in saying this he echoed the feeling of the great majority of hearers. Here is how James Denney ends a ser-

mon on the " Deadliness of Slander." " If you
have a suspicious temper fight against it; if you
think it clever to detect the quality of selfishness or vice behind the virtues of others, suspect
yourself; if you have any joy in the exposure of
unworthy methods, be afraid. But above everything, if you wish to be remote from the unpardonable sin, rejoice in the work of Jesus. Acquaint yourself with what is being done in His
name and in His spirit and power with the casting
out of evil spirits, with the preaching of the
Gospel to the poor, with the mighty works of
love which men and women inspired by Him are
doing in all the world; acquaint yourself with
these things, rejoice in them, promote them, give
thanks to God for them, and the thought of sin
against the Holy Spirit will never make you
afraid." Sometimes a very effective ending is
helped by a short, well-conceived illustration.
Thus James Reid concludes a sermon on " The
Triumph of Faith: " " Beside every *impasse* God
stands till we come up to it, waiting to work the
miracle, waiting to reveal Himself in the endowment of power. God never gives any man power
in reserve. We live only by the grace we are
forced to use. In the *Pilgrim's Progress*, Bunyan
puts this very clearly. Christian went out at
the secret bidding of his soul, with his face to the
light, went on till he fell into a slough across the

road; and being in it went on, still with his face to the light though he could see no way of getting out.   Then, and not till then, did he see the stretched-out hand of Help, who mysteriously came and mysteriously went — none other than the Holy Spirit Himself.   Only when we face tasks in His name which put a strain upon our faith, only then will rise within us the strength of God." [8]

The precise form in which the conclusion may be cast should not be stereotyped.   Various methods should be studied and used.   The preacher may end with an inference, an appeal, a suggestion, a short illustration, a prayer, a practical direction or a few pungent, searching questions. There are some who regret that the form of direct effective appeal is now a lost art, but it may be questioned whether its revival to general use is desirable.   Just as indirect suggestion is often better than direct suggestion, so an indirect appeal, if dexterously worded, is more effective and also more in harmony with modern taste and feeling. There are indeed rare occasions when under the influence of some startling event or situation national or civic, or after a more than usually earnest presentation of the Christian message, a direct, forcible and personal appeal may be right and fitting.   But only a man of known spirituality

[8] *The Victory of God*, pp. 221, 222.

of character can do it well. As an illustration of letting the peroration take the form of rhetorical questions, here is how Dr. R. J. Campbell as he draws to a close a sermon on " Self-examination " makes his " Application ": " Whither are you going? What is your life tending towards? Who is better or happier for your presence in this world? If you were to pass your motives and conduct in review for even one day, how much could you say was of Christ, and how much would you have to be ashamed of if all the world could see you as you are? . . . And conversely, how much is there in your ordinary state of heart that needs revolutionizing, how much evil to be cast out? What pain have you caused by your selfishness or thoughtlessness to those whom you have power to hurt only because they love you? " One feels, however, that even this able preacher falls into the error of overdoing a good thing, and in this sermon asks too many questions, no less than twelve!

The Abbé Bautain maintained that the best peroration, because the most simple and natural one, issues straight from the discourse and goes right to the soul of the listener. " Since you have spoken," he says " to gain some point, to convince and persuade your hearer, and thus influence his will by impressions and considerations, and finally, by some paramount feeling which must give the finishing stroke and determine him to action, the epitome of the ideas must be itself strengthened, and as it were, rendered living by a few touching words which inspired the feeling in question at the last moment so that the convinced and affected hearer shall be ready to do what is requested." [9] I would add another precept: Keep an imaginative touch for the end. The imagination is the last spiritual activity to be exhausted.

Whatever may be the method of our conclusion, we must take care that we know thoroughly the thought and even the language of which it is composed. Otherwise when we want to finish we cannot do it, and we weary our hearers by our abortive efforts to find a way of escape until at last we close with some commonplace that casts its shadow upon a discourse which but for this fatality might have left a good impression. Know then, where you are going to stop, and let no excitement generated by the act of speaking, no suggestion of a new idea, cause you to change your mind. The time for additions to your material is passed for good or ill. Beware of the fate of that preacher of whom it was said that in closing his discourse he executed a series of tacks across a Dead Sea of platitudes in the hope of entering the desired haven.[10]

[9] *Art of Extempore Speaking*, pp. 264, 265.
[10] See Appendix: Professor Niehergall on, " The Psychology of the Conclusion."

V

VARIOUS TYPES OF RELIGIOUS DISCOURSE

VARIETY is the spice of life; it is also the spice of sermons. It is a good thing, as we have already indicated, that the preacher should have for the main bulk of his sermon-output a consistent framework. And as we have also indicated, this framework is not a hard, rigid, mechanical scheme; it is, on the contrary, elastic, capable of being harmonized with great variation. There are times when the preacher will be called upon to abandon this type of sermon composition altogether for a type less elaborate and adapted to new circumstances and new demands. With the effort to meet the fresh situation will come a fresh delight in preaching.

1. The Expository Sermon

This form of pulpit address differs from the ordinary textual sermon in that, as a rule, instead of a text a considerable Scriptural passage is selected, as for example, a psalm, or an incident or a parable or several verses from an Epistle. Unhappily it has gone out of fashion. It was killed by the incompetence and laziness of the expositors who, it is to be feared, found it easy to make short comments on verse after verse, without any particular aim, and bored the congregation by a sort of milk and water decoction which eventually disgusted a healthy spiritual appetite. But there is such a thing as real expository preaching and I am in hearty accord with Dean Brown of Yale when he pleads so cogently for a revival of this forgotten form of edifying and instructive discourse.[1] The expository preacher selects a single text or more frequently a paragraph which is a unity in itself, and treats the various facts, with the details needed to explain them, so as to impress upon the congregation the central message of text or paragraph. Or, he may take an entire book, study its underlying idea or ideas, know it thoroughly in its historic background, the temporal circumstances through which the eternal message comes, and then expound it in systematic order, taking care to bring it into relation with the needs, the sins, the problems of the present day. Such a serious study might mark an epoch in the spiritual and intellectual history of a congregation, changing its convictions and deepening its apprehension of divine truth.

[1] *Art of Preaching*, pp. 32–61.

There are many advantages to be gained by this method and these more than pay for the increased labor which it costs the preacher. For one thing he subjects himself to the educational process. To be successful he must give himself to the mastery of the Bible. We all have our favorite books, and we neglect whole regions rich in un-mined ore, sacred treasure of the enjoyment of which we deprive not only ourselves but those who wait upon our ministry. Our age is an age of specialists and we ought to concede so far to the spirit of the time as to be authorities on certain Biblical books; this however is quite compatible with a sound working knowledge of all the rest. If there is any book of the Bible with which you are not familiar, you cannot do better than prepare to deliver a short course of expository lectures upon it. You cannot really expound the Bible unless its great underlying principles have got into your system and circulate in the blood and tissue of the soul.

It has another signal blessing for the preacher. The subject is given him for several weeks in advance; he is saved from the waste of energy involved in hunting about for a theme.

Moreover, this method educates the hearer. It acquaints him with the general and progressive tendency of revelation as a whole. He learns to distinguish between one prophetic message and another and how each stood related to the social and moral conditions of the age which gave it birth. He sees, possibly for the first time, the personalities of Holy Writ as men of like passions with ourselves, living, sinning, suffering, repenting, working, dying; and the ancient book becomes dynamic, dramatic literature. Still more: the old notion that the Bible is a magazine of proof texts, to be hurled at theological opponents, cannot persist under preaching of this order, since preacher and hearer alike feel the influence of the larger and humaner meanings of Scripture. " Hence the great doctrines of faith and prayer, of atonement, of regeneration, of inspiration, and all the great moral problems as well, are viewed in the light of Scripture, taken in the large. The people are delivered from the whole habit of judging the Bible by some strong sentence in it. the peddling, pelting use of texts is banished by this better method. The people are encouraged to put their trust in the general trend and drift of the Bible's teaching, to shape their belief and conduct by the main conclusions to which it brings them, and to develop their attitudes by the whole point of view which it gradually induces." [2]

To write a good expository lecture, a man must have among other gifts and acquirements a sound acquaintance with the Bible, a knowledge of the

[2] Brown, op. cit., p. 44.

history of religion and of the archaeological discoveries which have uncovered the civilizations
and literatures of Egypt, Assyria, Babylon, but
above all he must have spiritual insight and a
literary sense which can be gained only by a study
of the great masters of writing. To read the
glowing phrases of St. Paul, struck off in the white
heat of spiritual excitement as if they were so
many stones in a dogmatic structure is to misin-
terpret the Apostle and turn poetry into prose.

It has been wisely said that the best way of
preparing to expound the book of Job is to make
a close study of " Hamlet "; and the more one
knows of the great poetic masterpieces in our own
tongue, the better will he be prepared to interpret
the riches of Hebrew psalmist and prophet. But,
of course, you cannot afford to neglect the study
of those specimens of the art of exposition given
us by masters in that type of preaching, as for
example, Robertson's *Lectures on the Epistles
to the Corinthians*, Bradley's *Lectures on the
Book of Job*, Dale's *Lectures on the Epistle to
the Ephesians*, Bishop Gore's exposition of the
Sermon on the Mount, and of the *Epistles to the
Romans and to the Ephesians*, and such a brilliant
gem as G. A. Smith's exposition of the *twenty-
third psalm*.

2. Biographical Sermon-Lectures

There is perhaps no subject for sermons so much enjoyed by the average churchgoer as is the portraiture of the great men of the Bible. Here truth is seen embodied in flesh and blood. These ancient figures are no longer vague bodiless abstractions, they live and breathe and move before us and we feel our kinship with them in their sorrows, their sins, their repentances. We learn to know them and to love them as familiar friends. Some of them become our heroes whom we admire and in a measure imitate. " Ideas are poor ghosts that fill our sunlit eyes," as George Eliot says, " but personalities draw us as flame to flame." You will secure variety and increased interest if now and then you select one of the commanding figures of the Bible, divide his life into its chief epochs and re-tell his story with color and detail to be obtained by careful study of the appropriate sources.

In what book can we find such an assemblage of men and women, not figures of buckram and pasteboard but flesh and blood embodiments of mingled good and ill as the Bible offers us? The perennial attraction of these actors on the stage of Scripture lies in this that their histories are written, their characters portrayed, with a sureness of touch, a feeling for reality, in which many modern

religious biographies are singularly lacking. A
mingled earthliness and spirituality, years of commonplace, humdrum, prosaic happenings inter-
rupted at great moments by an incursion from the
other world, when God breaks silence with the
hero the levels of whose life are henceforth
shifted to a higher plane — such is the picture
which the writers draw and it is true to experience.
These old-world personages lived a twofold life,
a material and a spiritual, and hence we see in them
as in a mirror our very selves. The preacher with
an eye for psychological meanings can make character portraits so " moving delicate and full of
life," that they will reveal the modern man to
himself, lay bare the internal mechanism of his
soul, probe his consciousness, purify and ennoble
his whole being. What a profound impression
such preaching made upon the sensitive soul of
Amiel as he describes it in his *Journal!* He had
gone to hear Adolphe Monod, whose subject was
St. Paul as a pattern of the active life of the
Christian. " He made St. Paul *cry* during an hour
and a half; he made an old nurse of him, he
hunted up his old cloak, his prescriptions of water
and wine to Timothy, the canvas tent he mended,
his friend Tychicus — in short, all that would
raise a smile; and from it he drew the most un-
failing pathos, the most austere and penetrating
lessons. He made the whole St. Paul, martyr,

Apostle, and man live again before us, and this with a grandeur, an unction, a warmth of reality, such as I have never seen equalled. How stirring is . . . such an apotheosis of a human, natural, inbred Christianity, in an age, when some people think of it, so to speak, above man, and others below man! Finally, as a peroration, he dwelt upon the necessity for a new people, for a stronger generation, if the world is to be saved from the tempests which threaten it. 'People of God, awake! Sow in tears that ye may reap in triumph!' What a study is such a sermon! I felt all the extraordinary literary skill of it, while my eyes were still dim with tears. Diction, composition, similes, — all is instructive and precious to remember. I was astonished, shaken, taken hold of." [3]

Do you wish for guidance and help in the studies preliminary to the work of such pen portraits as well as in the technique of the art itself? You will find it in such a masterpiece as Renan's *The Apostles*, and in such excellent books as F. D. Maurice's *Kings and Prophets of the Old Testament* which is the best of Maurice's Biblical works, Matheson's *Representative Men of the Bible*, the various volumes in *Men of the Bible Series*, Stopford Brooke's *Old Testament in Modern*

[3] Amiel's *Journal* (Mrs. Ward's Translation) under Nov. 9, 1851.

Life, Dr. Alexander Whyte's *Bible Characters,* and Mr. F. B. Meyer's various studies in Biblical biography. Of course, such preaching becomes tedious and uninteresting unless the preacher takes care to relate his story so as to throw light upon the vital questions and interests of the present hour.

I would venture to suggest that to confine our expositions to the characters of the Bible is to narrow unduly the scope of the preacher's craft. Has not God been speaking to men through men in all the centuries? Has not the spirit of Christ incarnated itself in saints, reformers, teachers, prophets, missionaries, martyrs, evangelists throughout the Christian centuries? Only convention forbids the preacher to make one of these the theme of his address occasionally at least; and it is high time that in the interests of reality this convention should be set at nought. " Of good men it may be said it does us good only to look at them." An example in which mellowed wisdom and spiritual insight are wedded to abundant knowledge and much realism is to be found in *Sermons Biographical and Miscellaneous* by Benjamin Jowett. The second service in most of our churches presents an unpleasing spectacle. Why not try to solve the problem by a different form of pulpit address from that which is prescribed for the morning service, and what better topic would you find than the life of a Livingstone, a Pasteur, a Wesley or a Jonathan Edwards, a Charles Kingsley, an Abraham Lincoln or a William Booth on the anniversaries of their birthdays or as near as may be to them?

3. Ten Minute Sermons

At services which are in the main musical and devotional, and frequently the second service is or ought to be of this character, a brief sermon or address will be found suitable and greatly appreciated. Just because of its brevity preachers imagine that it requires less time and thought than more ample efforts, and they are tempted to palm off on their hearers either a bald summary of a longer discourse or one of the divisions deprived of extremities in both directions. The fact is far otherwise. Dr. Charles Eliot, the former President of Harvard University, is reported to have said that the most difficult intellectual exercise was the seven minutes service in the University Chapel on week day mornings. Just as the artist's hand is visible in a miniature as in a life-size portrait, or the literary craftsman's in the short story as much as in the long novel, the preacher-artist can throw all his powers into the preparation of the short sermon to such effect that many a hearer unable to bear the strain of a half hour's discourse will listen with joy and satisfaction for the briefer period.

If the short sermon is to make its mark, it must obey certain conditions. The preacher has no time for introductory material. He should announce his subject in the tersest terms possible, and then plunge into it at once. Waste no minute in elaborate explanations. One large simple idea considered in its practical bearings and its relation to everyday life, and worked out so as to make an appeal is amply sufficient. "The little sermon must be definite without being bare, concise without being cramped, and it must make simply and unerringly towards its mark." An excellent sample of the appreciation of these principles is seen in Robertson Nicoll's *Ten-Minute Sermons*, and suggestions or seed-thoughts in the development of which the young preacher might well practice himself, are plentifully supplied in the little book entitled *Reality and Religion*, by that truly spiritual teacher, Sadhu Sundar Singh.

4. Outline Addresses on Burning Questions

There is a growing demand from the few that it shall no longer be compelled to take from the pulpit whatever may be offered it, without comment or criticism. The day of authority is gone. Even the churches based on authority must make some concession to the time-spirit. As people listen to the preacher they sometimes disagree with him or suspect that his knowledge of the matter discussed is not as ample as it ought to be, or at least, cannot help desiring to have a chance to argue the question out with the speaker. Yet convention prescribes silence, and not even is any sound of dissent permitted to an over-burdened soul. The result is that sensible people go through the motions of listening to the preacher but decline to believe his utterances which may seem irrefutable yet are quite unconvincing, because not brought to grips with the thoughts in the hearer's mind. Is it too much to suggest that there should be, say, once a month a special form of evening service at which the preacher might well deliver an address outlining one of the vital questions of the hour, and then make way for frank and free discussion by the men and women present? If to the conservative-minded the ecclesiastical building would seem inappropriate for such debate, there is generally a parish house or other building to which the audience might be invited to go at the close of the devotional part of the service. What a splendid opportunity this open discussion forum would give the minister to discover what people are really thinking about! Henceforth sermons must deal primarily not with what the sermonizer is interested in but with what lies close to the heart and mind of the long-suffering occupant of the pew. And still further the preacher must set his mind alongside that of his hearers, they must get together, and there must be free access from mind to mind. We cannot ignore the fact that today there is a widespread suspicion that ministers are paid propagandists, engaged to teach the dogmas of this or that church and that therefore, as un-free agents their utterances must be taken with a grain of salt. Such a suspicion is fatal to the power of the pulpit. There is but one way by which it can be dissipated. The preacher must descend from the pulpit, cast aside the symbols of authority, and refusing to be content with " a fugitive and cloistered virtue unexercised and unbreathed," enter the open forum where he can explain and defend the truths which he has prophetically declared, as well as treat of subjects that can be more conveniently handled from the platform. Here is an opportunity for the preacher to bring the Gospel close to the practical and burning issues of the hour.

The Bearing of Evolution on Religion; The Claim of Christ and the Teaching of Other Religions; Christianity and Race Distinctions; the Abolition of War; Prohibition; Crime; Immigration; Eugenics; Christ's Message to Society; the Claims of Youth upon the Older Generation; the Value of the Bible; the Spiritual Basis of International Relations; the Reunion of the Churches; Science and the Life after Death; Science and Belief in Prayer; the Future of Christianity and the Cause of Missions. Such are some of the questions which might well be utilized by the preacher who in turn would listen to the opinions and judgments of the audience. Take for example the missionary propaganda. Behind it today are new motives, new energies and new encouragements. Of the eleven religions that have survived the conflicts of the past there are only two possible to civilized and cultured humanity, Buddhism and Christianity. Never were the prospects of the ultimate triumph of Christianity brighter than they are today. The preacher can do much to hasten that triumph, first by understanding the world-religions, and then by inspiring the Church to achieve her divine commission. Occasionally an expert might be called in to offer his matured reflections on the matter discussed. Can anyone doubt that this work of enlightenment is what the Church ought to be doing not for its own fellowship merely but for the entire community? To do this work effectively it is of vital moment that the preacher fully inform himself of the pros and cons of the subject for discussion before he ventures to commit himself in public to this or that position.

5. Mission Addresses

Here the preacher addresses himself specifically and directly to the " unconverted " or to those who once converted belong now to the " lapsed " classes.   Here also his appeal is to certain elements in his own congregation and parish, such as those " who are at ease in Zion," but also to the surrounding community and more especially to the irreligious and the non-Churchgoing people of the community.   Here the clergyman becomes in the fullest sense of the term an evangelist.   The place where he evangelizes may be his own Church, or in an assembly hall, or in a theatre.   The time may be at any season but it is a matter for rejoicing that Lent is now generally regarded by all Christian churches as an especial call to evangelistic effort among the unchurched classes.   The type of preaching to be used depends, of course, upon the aim in view, and here the aim is the awakening of the careless, the recall of those who have wandered from the fold of Christ, the searching of the conscience of those who have an outward form of religion but who know nothing of its joys or its power.

Obviously the truths to be set forth and urged upon heart and conscience are the most elementary and fundamental; the fact and consequences of sin, the power of faith, the love of God as seen in the character of Christ, the gospel as a redemptive force for the whole man, body, soul and spirit, and in all the relationships of life. The emotions to which the older evangelists appealed are no longer available; doubt as to the everlasting penalties of the other world is widespread. Moreover, except with the coarsest natures the appeal to fear has questionable value; it may excite hysteria, and it will often repel and disgust. Yet it may be doubted whether in our reaction against the untenable doctrines of future punishment we have not gone too far. Moralists will allow that within certain limits the consequences of an act should have their weight in determining the decisions of the will. Is it true that man lives after death? If he does not, the whole perspective of human life is altered; if he does, then one must ask: How stands that future existence related to existence here and now? Is the relation organic or accidental? Must it not be forever true not only in this world but in all worlds that " what a man soweth that shall he also reap." Shall not the blind here be also the blind there? A reasonable yet realistic presentation of this truth, verifiable in experience here and now, can pierce even the stoutest mail of the sinful heart. Preach to men that death ushers them into another world in which they shall know themselves as continuing a life lived here and with a memory whereby to claim past thoughts and deeds as their own, and will not reason, conscience, prudence conspire to force upon them the seriousness of life and existence, to summon them to turn, to repent and be saved? It is this reasonable and morally sound preaching about the effects of sin that we are in sore need of today.

But the greatest motive and the most alluring is not concerned with the future but with the present. The sorrow and pain which our sins inflict will come whether we will or not, often in this world, infallibly in the next, but we can here and now enter into fellowship with God and be at peace. This last thought should be central in all mission preaching. The drive should be made upon the will, the emphasis put upon the actual rising up of the soul and its return to the Father. Here there is full scope for the play of all the preacher's humanity; nor can he be more fitly occupied than in pleading with sinful men to give up their evil ways, to accept the divine offer of reconciliation, and to enter upon the life that is life indeed.

VI

THE PSYCHOLOGY OF PREACHING

1. THE PREACHER

"Most of the time we live outside ourselves, we perceive only a colorless phantom of our real ego . . . we perceive this real ego whenever by a resolute effort of reflection we detach our eyes from the shadow which follows us in order to enter into ourselves." So writes Bergson. And Coleridge had said the same thing before Bergson when he laments that the majority of mankind are nowhere greater strangers than at home, in the inner world of their nature. It is to this lack of self-knowledge that many failures in the pulpit are to be traced. A sermon may embody all the laws of homiletics. It may contain fine ideas, logically set forth, well illustrated and properly applied, and yet it may wholly fail to catch the attention of the congregation or to win their good-will. Why? The answer is to be found in recalling what preaching really is. Preaching is the oral communication of divine truth. The Christian message is, in the oft-quoted phrase of Phillips Brooks, "truth through personality," a principle of which perhaps he was himself the most signal illustration. Hence the effectiveness of a discourse depends on the presence of certain psychic factors in due measure and proportion. "The personality of the preacher back of the words makes the difference between a good sermon and a poor one, a difference not so easy to distinguish in a written discourse. One may speak of this as temperament, but temperament plus; it is the man as a whole, the balance of his powers and his methods. People are not tired of preaching, but only of certain styles of sermons and preachers. It is the personality which is not attractive. Rather than any particular truth or sermon, the chief thing that a man contributes is his tone — the influence of his personality; if that is lacking he is as booming brass or a clanging cymbal. Whether the minister feels the congregation or not, the congregation feels the minister." [1] If, therefore, we would be effective preachers we must study our own natures, remove the hindrances to effective self-expression, and concentrate all our powers on the highest notch of their possibilities. How can we hope to read the hearts of other men, if we have never read our own? This implies that like busy sculptors we must be constantly at work upon ourselves, as upon unhewn

[1] C. B. Cutten: *Psychological Phenomena of Christianity,* p. 478.

blocks of marble, chiseling and shaping our characters into the expressions of the Divine idea latent within us. We must not merely study that our knowledge may grow from more to more; we must keep aglow the fires of enthusiasm and of faith lest they die out; we must keep our hearts open to all the impulses of good that come, we know not how.

Philo maintains that only a good man can be an interpreter of God, "for properly speaking no wicked man can be inspired, inspiration being appropriate only, for a *wise* man." [2] Now the spiritual essence of a real sermon lies in the element of revelation, that is, in other words, the perception of spiritual truth. But even when our conscience assures us of our integrity, we need to know the prevailing characteristics of our mental life.

There are certain questions which the preacher should put to himself and answer. Is my mind of a severely, logical and philosophical type, or is it emotional and sentimental? Have I imaginative powers? Is my public speaking effective? And if not, why not? What kind of persons does my personality attract? What kind does it repel? Have I a rich or a meagre subconscious activity? Have I a sense of humor? Have I a strong will? Have I the oratorical impulse? Or is my

[2] Quis rer. div. sit. LXII. *Wise* meant to the Hebrew essentially *moral*.

nature cold and reserved? The introspection needed in answering these questions will result in an increasing knowledge of the human soul and a heightened sympathy with the weaknesses and deficiencies of our fellows. Let us examine, therefore, the psychological elements on which our preaching will depend for power and success.

1. The Influence of the Subconscious Mind in Preaching

The subconscious is a subject which is rarely considered by students of preaching, and yet here as in other spheres of mental activity it is of vital significance. Subconscious influence affects our every thought and motive. We have all puzzled over questions which seemed insoluble, and then suddenly when our minds were occupied with some trivial thought or fancy, a flash of light illumined our mental horizon and our difficulties vanished without any effort on our part. What a reinforcement to our powers would come to us if we could enlist the subconscious as an aid in our work of preaching! Before considering how this may be done, it is well to remember that too often the preacher's subconsciousness stands in his way, sets up all sorts of barriers, and denies any real transmissive function to his personality. It is a curious fact that some men when they enter the pulpit, cease to be their free, natural selves; they become stilted, unnatural and ineffective. A parishioner once told a distinguished clergyman that if he would only speak in the pulpit as he spoke at the dinner table, freely, naturally, spontaneously, his efficiency would be increased by one hundred per cent. He took the good advice and became one of the most successful preachers of his time. Even great pulpit orators have occasionally been self-inhibited. Matthew Arnold tells us in one of his letters how he was disappointed in hearing Henry Ward Beecher preach. He felt that the orator was held back from letting himself go in his usual manner by the fact that he had been informed of Arnold's presence in the congregation. How often lesser men are paralysed by fear, the dread of making mistakes, undue anxiety about their words and manner. Some are in bondage through these fears all their lifetime. It is by no means easy to get rid of mental and moral inhibitions; yet they must be swept away if the word is to have free course and accomplish its mission.

How is the self-inhibited preacher to be set free? (1) By the conviction that he speaks not of himself but as one sent by Another and a Higher. To cultivate this prophetic consciousness is to win the prophet's strength. "Take your position as the ambassador of Jesus Christ," says

Adolphe Monod, " sent by God to treat with sinful men; believe that he who sends you will not leave you to speak in vain; labor for the salvation of those whom you address as if it were your own . . . you will then tremble more before God and less before man. You will then speak with liberty. If our faith were perfect, we should scarcely be in more danger of falling into false or declamatory tones, than of men crying out to a drowning man to seize the rope which is thrown out to save him." [3] These words are true, but with many they may not prove themselves true at once. Again and again the preacher's faith will weaken, and he will leave the pulpit self-reproachful and unhappy. There is but one remedy. More courage, more resolution, more of the heroic determination that says, " I will no longer be in bondage to these miserable fears. I must shake off these cowardly impulses that hold me down. I will trust God and not be afraid."

(2) By prayer. Cultivate the prayer state. Quiet the soul in the presence of the Father. Let your prayers be of the most simple and most direct character, and chiefly for a share of His divine presence. This should be followed by the offering of the self, soul and body, to God to be used for His redeeming purposes; especially should such

[3] *Lectures on the Delivery of Sermons in Select Discourses*, edited by H. C. Fish and D. W. Poor.

a prayer be offered immediately before commencing to preach.

(3) By self-suggestion. Relax the body, inhale a few times quietly and deeply and suggest to yourself self-control, self-possession, freedom, peace and power. The few moments which the preacher usually has to himself before beginning the delivery of his discourse are, if rightly used, of the greatest value in making his work an inspiration and a joy.

It is now time to turn to the positive help which the subconscious can afford us. Bishop Boyd Carpenter tells of a Mr. Bucke who achieved considerable fame as a preacher, chiefly by his dependence on the richness of his subconsciousness. " He was at his best when he took a subject and let it lay hold of his soul, and then, having selected a few clear lines of thought, let himself go. Then he would speak in a kind of rapture, like one falling into a trance and having his eyes open. The mind was detached from the circumstances of the moment. The subconscious mind was yielding up its stores of memory and illustration. Then he would fling out choice and witty sentences, the full force of which he did not himself realize at the moment. The strange part of the matter was this: he was afterwards depressed and almost despairing, complaining that he had made a mess of it and talked like a fool.

The truth was that he was so much the rapt
speaker that he had no power to measure what he
had said or how he had said it; and yet he had
uttered sentences of great power, flung out imagery, striking and suggestive, and now and again
a piece of real wit. On one occasion he was preaching on Balaam's ass, and in the course of his sermon said: 'There are some people who don't
believe that Balaam's ass spoke: I am of opinion
that it did, and what is more, *that a great many
asses have spoken since.*' Such an utterance was
not prepared beforehand. It was due to the action
of the subconscious mind which in such preaching
is called vividly into play." [4]

George MacDonald, poet, novelist, and preacher, affords the most remarkable illustration known
to me of this mysterious, creative faculty of mind.
It was my signal privilege in the early days of
my ministry to hear him preach. Certainly there
was nothing in the environment of the speaker
to commend his utterances to the auditor. A
dimly lighted, ugly, dingy chapel in the North of
London, the performances of the choir anything
but uplifting and exhilarating, nowhere an object
on which the eye could rest with aesthetic satisfaction. But as soon as the preacher began his
sermon, those things were forgotten; the quality
of " grip " manifested itself from the start. In

4 *Some Pages of My Life*, pp. 316, 317.

simple, beautiful conversational English, with an occasional lift of the voice at the bidding of a swelling emotion or of an emphatic appeal, he poured fourth apparently without effort a stream of noble thoughts and gracious sentiments which woke responsive echoes in my heart. The audience gathered from all parts of the metropolis was held in the hollow of his hand. On the same day I had heard Dr. Westcott in Westminster Abbey, and Mr. Spurgeon in his Tabernacle, but good as their sermons were, it was George Mac-Donald that made an impression which the lapse of years has failed to efface. I have often wondered since what was, from a psychological point of view, the secret of his fascination. In a private letter from Dr. MacDonald's distinguished son, Dr. Greville MacDonald (which he kindly permits me to quote) he goes far to reveal the secret. " My father," he writes, " did not study the subject of preaching at all, his own delivery being so unusually spontaneous. Beyond having a quiet hour with his subject on every occasion when he was to lecture or preach, he made no preparation and no notes. When I was with him in the States in 1872, I heard him lecture about forty times on Robert Burns, and I used to declare that never once did he give us the same lecture. So it was with his preaching." Here unquestionably is an evidence of an unusual activity of the subconscious.

Most preachers will place, and rightly place, their main dependence on their conscious powers. The question is: Can they utilize the forces of the subconscious with a view to the more efficient use of their personality? The answer is: They can. First of all, when we choose a subject and allow our minds to work on it for a little, we should then turn away from conscious thinking about it for a space, hand it over to the subconscious activity and let it undergo a process of gestation. Without our being aware of it, ideas, sentiments, similes, illustrations will gather round it, and when we sit down to the work of writing the sermon we shall find our task greatly lightened. When the sermon is finished it should be worked into the very texture of the mind, so that it may become part of our subconscious activity. The best method for accomplishing this is, after the completion of the sermon and after revision and several careful readings, to relax the body, close the eyes, quiet the mind and recall very gently the main lines of thought and especially the links of connection, repeating them over and over again. When you stand in the pulpit you will be astonished and delighted at the ease and freedom which will characterize your speech. The power to enjoy this experience differs, of course, in different men, but it is possible, in a measure, to all. Here lies the secret of what has been called " psychic

power in preaching." For want of it learned, eloquent, polished discourses pass us by without
leaving a trace upon our souls; where it energizes,
a man may break all the technical rules of his art
and yet prove a mighty power. There is a tremendous electric potency stored in the human soul
when kept in harmony with God's will and made
the channel of His vital purpose. And such a soul
guided by clear intellectual perceptions of its task
and moved by a powerful emotion, constitutes a
psychic power which mere marshalling of logic or
rhetorical art cannot produce. The imperative
need of the preacher is to set free this " electric
potency " so that, thrilling with his message, the
hearer may catch the contagion of his passion.

But certain conditions must be obeyed as you
stand up to deliver your message. First, get rid of
all bodily tension. Do not clench the hand, or
clutch any part of your dress. Stand not stiffly, but
at ease and in a relaxed posture. This physical
attitude will have a reflex influence on the mind
and will contribute to an essential in all effective
public speaking, that is, poise of personality. As
the preacher's whole being is thus free from strain,
not only will the subconscious give up its treasures,
but the mind will be sensitive to the impressions
coming from the congregation, and that subtle
interchange of thought and feeling between
speaker and hearers so vital to real preaching

will be sustained and developed. It is under these conditions that inspired moments visit the preacher. Then it is that there are " uprushes from the subliminal " which carry the preacher, as the saying goes, beyond himself, that is, beyond his ordinary, normal self, and impress the hearer with the fact that he is listening to an inspired utterance. Then it is that he lets himself go, yet has himself under control; personality meets personality, soul mingles with soul, and for the moment preacher and audience are fused into absolute unity of feeling. One of the reasons of the decadence of pulpit influence today is the great infrequency of such an experience.

Is it necessary here to utter a word of warning? The subconscious is no substitute for hard work: it cannot produce what it does not possess. Out of nothing, nothing comes. Only that man can have a richly furnished subconsciousness who has thought, and felt, who has grappled with hard questions, and has imaginatively brooded upon the undying quests of the soul. Some men depend on the subconscious to the neglect of conscious and severe self-cultivation, with the consequence that they become empty sentimentalists, the creators of an emotional speech that appeals only to the weak-minded and the tearful.

2. The Influence of the Will in Preaching

" The living force of the human soul brought to bear upon living souls for the sake of their transformation is the fundamental idea of preaching." [5] Observe that this description of preaching is in terms of the *will*. This is in harmony with the modern tendency to regard the will as the primary and constitutive function of the mind. A man may have a good intelligence, a sympathetic heart, and a desire to do good, but if he is deficient in will-power, his speech will lack driving force. It is the will that enables a man to project his thoughts and aspirations into the minds of others. The battle is half won as soon as the preacher resolves that the hearers must listen; but this resolution implies, of course, a forthgoing of volitional power. " The preacher should be a man of *strong will*. A strong will is one in which powerful impulses are subject to an equally powerful self-control. The impulsive and inhibitive factors of personality should balance one another; but both must be strong to make a strong will. The greatest public speakers have been notable in this respect. Their powerful impulses enable them to stir an audience; but their equally powerful self-restraint, while making the impression of reserved force, checks unhealthy excesses.

[5] Beecher: *Yale Lectures,* p. 13.

They make a balanced and proportional appeal to the emotional and intellectual faculties of their hearers. They react with great energy upon their audiences, but they react upon the *whole* nature of those under their influence." [6]

Individuals differ in the range of their will-power; but the fact to be emphasized is that will-power can be cultivated and strengthened. Its foundations are sound health, a well-balanced nervous system, and a disciplined mind. The centre of the will is the power of attention. Hence habits of inattention and mind-wandering sap the very basis of volitional energy. One of the best ways of strengthening the will is to attend to what ever has the right to claim your attention at the moment. It was said of Gladstone that whether it was a speech he was delivering or a game he was playing or an interview he was giving, his whole personality was completely absorbed in the matter in hand, as if he had no other interest whatsoever. The activity of the will, be it remembered, is as much concerned with the compulsive ordering of the preacher's words in the pulpit as with the building of the sermon in the study. You may have an excellent sermon intellectually considered, but it will evoke a very languid assent unless driven home by vigorous psychical qualities in yourself. Your words must not only transmit thoughts, they

[6] Gardner: *Psychology and Preaching*, p. 206.

must convey emotional energy. For genuine preaching is, at bottom, a struggle of will with will. Unless the will of the hearer is carried, the sermon is a failure. In the pulpit the preacher must gird up the loins of his soul to a life grapple with the congregation by a calm, steady pressure of the will to bring heart and mind to the acceptance of his message. The sermon must be a deed as well as a word. The preacher must *will* the good of those to whom he speaks.

3. The Imagination in Preaching

A recent writer on the art of preaching classes the imaginative quality of a sermon among its lighter elements. This is to confound fancy with imagination. Fancy deals with odd or curious or superficial relations of objects. It is wayward, capricious, dividing, and plays upon the mere surface of things. Imagination is the faculty by which we are able to visualize the invisible, to present it in such concrete form that men feel it as reality. " The imagination sees. Out of material stored in the mind it creates a living world. By its forces the Parthenon is no longer a ruin and the Greeks yet live. The imagination gives atmosphere and stimulates individual ideas. Mere facts may make a wrong impression, but imagination clothes facts with living scenes and situations and presents the hidden truth. Imagination is the basis of all figurative language. It compares object with object, identifies the unknown and the known, and creates a new whole." [7] The main function of the preacher is to imagine unseen realities and to reveal them to others in such a way that they shall be as convincing as things seen with the bodily eye. It is only through the imagination that the emotions can be stirred. Abstractions, however lofty, cannot move the feelings. A speaker may feel deeply the truth he is expounding, he may even choke with the pressure of his emotions, and his hearers may remain calm and unmoved. Why? Because only through distinct images can the emotions be touched. The newspaper reporter knows this, and therefore he hurries over the general features of the tragic occurrence which he describes and concentrates on the sufferings of the victim and the reactions of the spectators. " Not our logical, but our imaginative faculty is king over us," says Carlyle. We can transmit our emotional tone to another only through the medium of imagination. Take the subtlest or the most sublime thought, present it in pictorial form, or in the guise of a striking illustration, and even the untrained, average man will understand and feel.

The mental images which form, so to say, the

[7] S. S. Curry: *Foundations of Expression,* p. 145.

preacher's stock in trade are of various types corresponding to the senses affected, such as visual, auditory, motor, tactile images. It is important for the preacher to discover the prevailing cast of his mental imagery. The great poets and orators use frequently the imagery of the various types mentioned, but at the head of the list for frequency stand visual images. A student of Tennyson has discovered that in a thousand lines of his *Idylls of the King*, the poet used eighty-three visual, forty-eight auditory, one motor and seven tactile images. I have examined a sermon by Robertson and one by Brooks, each consisting of about four thousand words, and have found that Robertson used thirteen visual, four auditory, three motor and three tactile images, whereas Brooks uses fifteen visual, seven auditory, eight motor and two tactile images. Rich as is the Englishman in imagery, the American is still richer. It is now known that visual images make the most general appeal.

> "The business of the drama must appear
> In action or description. What we hear
> With slower passion to the heart proceeds
> Than when an audience views the very deeds."
>   (Horace: *Ars Poetica*.)

Hence the advice to give the teacher is equally good for the preacher. "Work for the picture."

All the influential preachers whose sermons are available have been characterized by a strong picture-forming faculty. Especially today, when millions witness moving picture plays daily and are unconsciously acquiring thereby a disposition of mind which makes them impatient of truth that is not vividly set forth in pictorial form, must the preacher translate principles and doctrines into scenes, situations, visions. Anything that cannot be so translated cannot be of vital import.

Several practical conclusions follow. The preacher should aim at gaining as large a stock of visual images as possible, but he must not confine himself to these. Different forms of imagery relieve the monotony produced by the use of a single form. The imagination can be developed. The preacher should cultivate the power to recall what he has experienced, in visual, concrete images, and he can do this only by close, concentrated attention. Imagination is a universal possession of humanity in a more or less degree. Geniuses possess it in an abnormal degree. Bunyan and Newman saw the abstractions of the spiritual world in concrete forms " like men walking in the street." Special gifts make the formation of mental images easier for one man than for another. The fact remains, however, that valuable results can be obtained by resolution and work. How is this form to be described? (1) By keen observance of the beautiful things of nature, and the choicest products of the plastic and pictorial art. (2) By close study of poetry and drama. The poet and the dramatist from the nature of their craft use a language which is higher, more emotional, more intense than that of ordinary prose. If they would succeed they must deal in pictures and visions, and in suggestive hints that spur the imagination of the reader. Dante, Shakespeare, Milton, Shelley, Wordsworth, Tennyson, Browning, Matthew Arnold, and among the minor bards William Watson, Francis Thompson and Rudyard Kipling, are of special value to the preacher. There is another still deeper reason why the proclaimer of the Gospel should steep his mind in the best poetry. The late Professor Denney wrote to a clerical friend: " It was delightful to hear that you were going in for reading the poets through. The longer I live the more I feel the truth of Aristotle's doctrine that poetry is more philosophical than history; it is a higher kind of truth, and indeed the only form in which the highest kind of truth can get even imperfect expression." Fiction, too, though in a much less degree, helps the creative function of the imagination. But it has been pointed out that it leaves the reader too passive; the scenes and situations depicted by the novelist pass before the reader's eyes; he is a spectator and enjoys the pictures as they pass, but he is not forced to contribute anything to stir up his imaginative powers in order to see and utilize what else would escape him. Fiction has its value for the preacher which has been indicated elsewhere, but there are better instruments for the stimulation of his creative powers.

4. The Emotions of Preaching

What is the place of emotion in preaching? This is a question with which the man who preaches must come to terms, if his work is to be crowned with success. In the prevailing reaction of the pulpit against vapid sentimentalism, we are in danger of falling into the other extreme of over-intellectualism. Dr. A. E. Garvie rightly remarks: " The failure of a great deal of preaching to be fully effective is due to its being too intellectualistic. The preacher is conveying only ideas and ideals from his own to another's reason and conscience, but he is not communicating the passion or enthusiasm he himself may feel. Without weak sentimentalism and violent emotionalism effective preaching does demand that there shall be warmth as well as light." [8] The sermon must be addressed not exclusively to this or that function of the soul, but to the whole moral and reli-

[8] *The Christian Preacher,* p. 12.

gious personality. But it cannot be so addressed, unless it comes from the entire consecrated personality of the preacher. This accounts for the fact that an old sermon which once had a powerful appeal, no longer meets with any response. The old ideas no longer call forth in the preacher's own heart the same sincere and deep feeling. On the other hand, the emotions must be controlled by reason and intelligence. Says S. T. Coleridge: " Every attempt in a sermon to cause emotion, except as the consequence of an impression made on the reason and understanding or the will, I hold to be fanatical and sectarian." [9] The uneducated man, owing to the unchecked quality of his emotional life, can produce by suggestion striking emotional manifestations in others, whereas the cultivated man whose emotions are under the control of his intellect will produce less excitement on his hearers, but he will make a deeper and more vital impression. The culture of the religious life should tend more, not to suppress the emotions, still less to kill them, but to control them and crystallize them through moral activity. [10]

If we consult the great orators, we shall find that they unanimously concur in holding that emotion is essential to the highest oratory. " I frankly confess," says Cicero, " that I owe my success much

[9] *Table Talk*, p. 203.
[10] See Gardner: *Psychology and Preaching*, pp. 288, 289.

less to my own efforts than to the force of the passions which agitate me when I speak in public. It was this force which enabled me to reduce Hortensius to silence, and to close the mouth of Catiline." And again: " It is not possible for the hearer to grieve or hate or fear or be moved to commiseration unless the emotions which the speaker wishes to communicate are deeply impressed upon himself and stamped on his own bosom with characters of fire." So well do great actors know this fact, that in order to arouse in themselves the feeling which they wish to convey to the audience, they work up the emotions before appearing on the stage by visualizing the particular scene in whch they are to take part or in listening to the dialogue which the other actors are carrying on. If we turn to the great preachers, we hear their united testimony that they must be touched themselves before they can touch others. Dr. A. V. G. Allen, writing of Phillips Brooks, says: " He first opened his soul to the influence of the truth which was to constitute his message, devising the most forcible method in order to make it appeal to his own heart. He studied its effect upon himself before studying how to reach his congregation." Read any sermon by J. H. Jowett, or Beecher, or Robertson, or W. E. Orchard (the sermons of this last are preëminently intellectual), and you will find an emotional quality which gives the truth enunciated driving energy. The emotions of joy and sorrow, pathos and awe dispose the mind to accept the ideas and ideals of the sermon, and open up a way to win the motives and so control the will. Without deep feeling on the part of the speaker, it is impossible for him to impart to the discourse that accent of conviction which is the secret of all successful preachers.

Some preachers are ashamed of enthusiasm or fervor in their delivery. It may be that this is the reaction against an excessive sentimentalism which repels all manly minds. But the abuse of a good thing does not forbid its use. The absence of any expression of emotion leaves upon the hearers the impression that the speaker is discharging a perfunctory duty in which he is not greatly interested. And this, of course, is a foolish mistake. We can easily detect the false emotion, the emotion that is aroused or is allowed to run free from restraint and show itself in declamatory tones. Avoid as you would a plague what is known as "tears in the voice" or an artificial tremolo. It only irks and frets the hearer. But there is a noble emotion generated by noble ideas which every preacher ought to cultivate. This emotional spontaneity, born of great ideas by which the speaker has become possessed, will give a touch of passion to his speech in which his entire personality will be released to work its effect upon the congregation. Moreover, the great mass of men are impatient of abstract reasoning. William Sunday knows this elementary fact, hence he can crowd his mammoth tent with an intensely interested audience of thousands whom he sways from tears to laughter at the bidding of his own powerful emotions. There is a reservoir of potential energy within the average man which the popular evangelist knows how to tap, but which the pastoral preacher neglects with great loss to his effectiveness. After all, it is not mere thought he has to communicate, it is *vital force*.

A few practical hints may be added.

1. Do not " tear a passion to tatters " — which means, do not rant and declaim, do not permit bodily movements beyond what is appropriate for that degree of emotion which you feel at the time.

2. Do not make any gestures with the arms as expressing emotion, without any accompanying movement of the muscles of the face. Some preachers never change the facial expression, while they use freely, arms and hands. And yet facial expression is the first and most important manifestation of emotion.

3. Do not begin a sermon with any expression of emotion which implies pain or sorrow. The audience is not yet in sympathy with you, and is more or less critical. You must win them by an emotion born of an agreeable thought.

4. While strong convictions deeply felt are essential to the preacher, do not fall into the sin of overcharging your sermons with personal convictions so that you give the auditors the feeling that you are arrogating solely to yourself the merit of possessing any convictions at all.   A sympathetic imagination which identifies you with your hearers will make this fault impossible.

VII

THE PSYCHOLOGY OF PREACHING

2. The Hearer

1. The Psychology of the Hearer

ALL really effective preaching depends not only on what the preacher gives the congregation but on what the congregation gives the preacher. There is a subtle interchange of thought and feeling: without it, the speaker is simply beating the air. By a kind of sixth sense the best speakers can feel the spiritual pulse of their audiences, and can relate themselves to it so as to bring about the desired result. But there is more than this in the relation of speaker and hearer. "There is an instinctive sympathy which may always be relied upon. The high tuning of the speaker's own spirit perforce awakens sympathetic chords and tends to attune the spirit of his audience. There are times when we can see more than we can picture in words. But the audience may still see with us. We impart to them our visions; because they may be and often are attuned to receive them. Hence a preacher need scarcely, ever regret the things he didn't say. These are providential omissions; and there are equally providential seizures by the minds of the congregation of the influence and benediction of the things which heightened the preacher's own spirit, though he himself may not be aware of having given them expression." [1]

It follows that the first problem of the preacher is to secure the attention of the hearer as an indispensable basis of the condition of *rapport* between them. If indeed the hearer cultivated the right conditions of hearing, that is, if he cultivated a sense of the reality and importance of worship, the preacher's task would be greatly lightened. But consider the mental state of an average congregation as compared with that of an assembly listening to a political oration or a scientific lecture. Or contrast the churchgoer with the citizen in the jury box who hearkens carefully to the testimony of the witnesses and to the utterances of the counsel and the judge. Dean Swift in a celebrated sermon on " Sleeping in Church " draws a picture of how people regarded sermons in his day. His caustic criticism is not altogether out of date, though convention prescribes today a more polite behavior. " Men whose minds are much enslaved to earthly affairs all the week, cannot disengage or break the chain of their thoughts so suddenly as to apply to a discourse that is wholly

[1] Mark: *Pedagogics of Preaching*, pp. 81, 82.

foreign to what they, have most at heart. Tell a
usurer of charity or mercy and restitution, you talk
to the deaf; his heart and soul and all his senses
are yet among his bags and he is grossly asleep and
is dreaming of a mortgage. Tell a man of business that the cares of the world choke the good
seed; that we must not encumber ourselves with
much serving; that the salvation of his soul is the
one thing necessary — you see, indeed, the shape
of a man before you, but his faculties are all gone
off among his clients and papers, thinking how to
defend a bad case or to find flaws in a good one;
or he weareth out the time in drowsy nods." The
preacher has to gain and hold the attention of
minds too often preoccupied with this, that, or the
other — anything and everything except the matter in hand. So difficult is his art that some
preachers have recourse to sensational methods.
The weakness of sensationalism is that it centres
the attention upon the speaker himself or upon his
device rather than upon the message he is there to
deliver.

Attention, the direction of consciousness this
way and not that, may be produced by three kinds
of causes. (1) *Compulsory attention.* This is the
attention which, excited by some cause from without, forces itself into the centre of consciousness.
A thunder clap, a sharp twinge of toothache, or a
painful piece of news compels attention. Now

the preacher may act as a stimulus of that sort. His manner or his intonation may be so unpleasing that he attracts attention, indeed, but only to prejudice his hearers against him. And on the contrary it may be so charming that they are won against their will to listen and enjoy. It is this last type of preaching you wish to practice. In order to achieve it, compulsory attention is not the kind you should desire because it directs the thought of the hearer from the message to the speaker and all preaching which does this is bad.

(2) *Voluntary attention.* Here the mind is directed toward a given subject by an effort of the will. If you could see into the minds of your hearers, what would you behold? A stream of thoughts flowing according to no law that can be detected. Ever-varying combinations of thoughts preoccupy the field of consciousness. The business of the preacher is to break in upon these preoccupations, to turn the hearer's attention from them by focusing it upon one object to the exclusion of all else. The attention thus gained is voluntary attention. It implies a certain effort on the part of the hearer; and continued mental effort is disagreeable. Hence the preacher should make only a modest claim upon *voluntary* attention. His message should be so presented that the strain implied in voluntary attention may be reduced to a minimum. The truths of religion are

so serious, so profound that it may seem impossible to avoid inflicting on the hearer a measure of irksome strain, if they are to be accepted and believed. It is here that preaching justifies its claim to be considered an art and a fine art. The preacher must so invest these truths with charm and attractiveness that the heart is thrilled and an enthusiastic love of them springs up spontaneously.

(3) *Spontaneous attention.* This comes when some interest dominates the mind and excludes all else. When we are free to think as we please, when the mind is not under the direction of the will, we give spontaneous attention to certain thoughts and desires. And these objects of thought are a true index to the type of character which we have cultivated. It is clear that the preacher should aim at winning the *spontaneous* attention of his congregation. And this is one of his greatest difficulties. For often the interest of the hearer is opposed to the preacher's message and this interest must be overcome by another which is on the side of the preacher. How can this be done? First of all, the subject should in itself be interesting and vital. A fatal homiletical sin is that of previously concerning yourself with the wrong material. Perhaps you have been reading the latest popularization of science and your sermon grows eloquent about ether, ions and electrons; or you are greatly interested in the

latest theory of the authorship of the Epistle to the Hebrews and you put the theory into a sermon. But your audience may not have the faintest interest in these things. Find out what your people are thinking about, what they feel to be of concern to their moral and spiritual life, and give this the central place in your preaching. Moreover, not all subjects connected with the Bible are suitable for preaching. " Better keep to daily experience, the bird's song, the children's laughter, the tragedy of life, the love of God. Human nature is the preacher's workshop." The really important themes for the preacher are those that come home to the business and bosoms of men, and if rightly presented, they will hold the hearer as the Ancient Mariner held the wedding guest, with an awe-struck and fascinated attention.

Then do not despise a touch of dramatic strategy. Spurgeon used to say to his students: " Cultivate the surprise power, leap into your subject, let your first sentences have something striking in them, vary your speed, dash like lightning, move calmly like the flowing river, use the bass notes, the clarion notes, be conversational, be dramatic, have variety, that is what human nature craves." If you are conscious that your sermons tend to be flat and dull, you should practice reading dramatically Shakespeare or Bernard Shaw, and you should take every opportunity, when telling a story, to tell it with as much animation and histrionic skill as possible. The dramatist gets his greatest effects by appealing to simple and universal feelings. So too with the preacher. The congregation contains persons of every stage of culture, of every degree of sensibility. But there are sentiments which appeal to all, as for example, love of freedom, need of companionship, justice, patriotism, mercy, love, self-sacrifice, courage. The preacher is like an organist, he has a whole diapason of motives on which to play.

Nor should we forget the power of choice diction to delight and fascinate the mind. Cicero said that the orator ought to have *almost* the diction of the poets. Some words are harsh and strike unpleasantly on the ear. So too with sentences; they may be quite grammatical but also quite unrhythmical. Harmonious speech is one of our most powerful weapons wherewith to overcome the indifference of the hearer. While aiming at graceful, beautiful speech be careful to avoid monotony. A sing-song tone in preaching is fatal to interest. When in delivering a sermon you feel yourself falling into this lamentable fault, there is but one remedy. Change the pitch of the voice and vary the tone in harmony with the specific quality of the thought expressed. Do not try to cure monotony by the physical act of shouting or by any artificial manipulation of the voice.   Speak as you would if you were having an interesting conversation with a friend.   Practice in your study the art of passing from the abstract to the pictorial, from generalities to details, from assertions to questions, from a quick dramatic speech to slow deliberate utterance or to a significant pause.   Interest in the sermon will also be maintained if we bear in mind that the hearer's attention is not uniform, but comes and goes in waves, some short, some long.   Psychologists tell us that the sentence should correspond to a single pulse of the attention.   Hence long and involved sentences are out of place in a sermon; they demand too great an interference with the laws of attention.   On the other hand, there is nothing more tedious than a series of short, jerky sentences; there must be variety in the length and form of the sentences.

Perhaps the greatest enemy of attention is " unreality in conception."   It is told of Joseph Chamberlain that on one occasion he converted an oratorical failure into a striking success.   He began a well prepared speech delivered from notes. The delivery was good, the speech was able and thoughtful, but he read failure on the faces of his guests and he saw that something was wrong. He threw his notes on the table and launched into a passionate description of the poor of Birmingham.   At once his hearers began to listen and his words were received with enthusiasm. *His speech had become real.* Have you ever noticed that in listening to a sermon, your attention is now caught, now lost? Something in the sermon at the outset grips you, but after a while your mind wanders, to be recalled later by some return of power to the thought or the words of the preacher. We ought to study the causes of this experience. One cause may be that the preacher has diverged to a side-path from the main avenue of his thought and in this side-path we are not interested. This of itself, even though his eloquence is unabated and his manner unchanged, suffices to break the spell. Another cause may be that the preacher has struck upon a line of thought with which he was not thoroughly familiar, with the result that a vagueness obscures his speech and our attention flags.[2] This is why people complain of being bored by sermons. Boredom springs no doubt, sometimes from religious indifference or from sheer mental frivolousness, but too often it is a state of mind generated by the preacher's inability to so present his thoughts that they seize and hold the attention. Not infrequently it is induced by the fact that having been bored before as we listened to the preacher we expect to be bored again,

[2] See O'Dowd: *Preaching*, pp. 45, 46. I desire to express my acknowledgments to this Roman Catholic writer for several valuable suggestions.

and our expectation is not likely to be disappointed. On the other hand, when the speaker knows his business, the heart beats quicker, a sense of comfort and satisfaction steals over us and half an hour vanishes with the rapidity of fifteen minutes. Our mental activity has been kept awake and we have been taken out of ourselves. Some preachers achieve the boredom of their hearers by such minute explicitness that the mind is left with nothing to do, or by a monotonous appeal to one element of the soul, intellect or conscience or feeling, leaving whole regions of the inner life impoverished. The secret of making tedium in the hearer impossible is — touch the various chords of his soul, do not overstrain any one of them. A shrewd lawyer talked with me once about preaching. " Tell me quite frankly," said I, " what you demand in a sermon." He replied, " When I listen to a sermon I want to be taken out of myself. I want to be lost in the ideal. Not commonplaces, not such things as I can get in newspapers and magazines, but something I can strive after and feel happy in so doing; — that is what I want." The only cure for unreality in thought is a thorough mastery of the sermonic material, and by adapting the discourse to the capacity and aptitudes of the audience.

I have emphasized the importance of the form of the sermon, but of far greater moment is the substance. The Archbishop of Canterbury has recently complained of the " thinness " of English preaching and his words are as applicable to America as to England. " You have no idea," writes a thoughtful man in a private letter, " the sort of stuff that is served up to us in the country churches of New England." Real thought means thought that is definitely and clearly conceived. Resolutely fix the mental eye upon the ideas you desire to communicate and do not rest content until all vagueness and superficiality are dissipated. Having seen the truth clearly for yourself, you will be able to make your hearers see it. They will attend.

But attention becomes difficult, if too prolonged. It is, therefore, necessary to give the hearer mental breathing-spells now and again. For example, if you are conducting a closely reasoned argument, you can rest the audience by interjecting an interesting anecdote or illustration; and after this brief relaxation you can easily grip them again. The congregation must not be kept in a state of tension for more than a brief period at a time. Allow the congregation a chance to slacken the attention for a short space, and the refreshment thus enjoyed disposes the hearer to listen to what follows. To sum up: if we deal with *living issues in a living way*, we need have no fear of want or weakness of attention on the part of congregations.

Few hearers are trained to attend, and the task of winning and holding their attention is nearly altogether the work of the preacher. You will do well, therefore, to study your audience, and if one method of expression does not succeed in awakening their spontaneous attention and in holding it, boldly cast that method aside and try another. On the other hand, do not be haunted with the notion that your hearers are able or ought to remember the whole of your sermon. A highly educated man who attended church regularly told a clerical friend of mine that all he asked from any one sermon was a single stimulating or inspiring or suggestive thought. " No educated man," he said, " can swallow whole the sermon of any preacher, nor is it desirable that he should. After all the note of a real sermon is something in it which sets the hearer thinking and thinking to some practical purpose."

The next problem in the psychology of the hearer is that of *psychical fusion*. At first hearers are self-centred, they have little common feeling. How is this isolation to be overcome? Here we can learn a lesson from the popular revivalist. You will notice that he always likes his audience to be crowded together. The reason is that this crowding together tends to reduce their sense of individuality. They cannot move freely and therefore the consciousness of self is lessened and this helps to unify their mental attitude. The first step in the process of fusing your audience is to invite them to get together. It is also worth noting that owing to the deep-rooted conservatism of some of our church officials the high pulpits of former days have been retained and the preacher is lifted up to an absurd height and so cannot get sufficiently near his audience.

But mere physical proximity is not enough; psychical powers must be brought to bear. A common feeling is generated by imaginative passionate speech. If the preacher can convey his ideas and emotions by vivid images and dramatic action he can convert a cold and critical congregation into a fused and receptive mass. "True oratory is reason animated by human interest — essential truth endowed with new life." Still another stimulant to fusion is congregational singing. Why? Because it appeals to the emotions, and assists in breaking down the barrier that caste or education or custom is continually building up. It creates the psychological atmosphere in which the powers of persuasion will work most efficiently. And it is persuasion that is the grand aim of preaching. "We persuade men," says the Apostle. Persuasion implies the presentation of reasons to the intelligence so that the hearer's choice may be a truly moral one. A mere appeal to passion or prejudice — a besetting sin of the pulpit — is disastrous for the spiritual life. It is not too much to say that if preachers keep steadily before them the power to persuade as the highest of all gifts, the influence of the pulpit would be immensely augmented.

The qualities which go to make a persuasive speaker are to be specially noted, for only by cultivating them can the preacher hope to gain his object. The gift of persuasion is partly a matter inherent in the unique character of the individual, partly the fruit of one's outlook upon life, partly the result of a truly spiritual apprehension of the Gospel, and partly, a matter of diction, at once clear, pure, harmonious and beautiful. All these qualities endow the preacher with that indefinable but priceless something which we call " charm." A cynic or a pessimist, who has no real belief in the spiritual nature of man can hardly expect to exercise a persuasive influence over the hearts of men. Nor will a harsh or belligerent preacher succeed in drawing his hearers into the Kingdom of God. The biographer of Boyd Carpenter says of him: " His attitude was essentially winning and persuasive, — that of an ambassador for Christ bearing glad tidings rather than a Hebrew prophet denouncing judgment." Dr. J. H. Jowett in an address delivered to a body of preachers laid down that all effective preaching must sound " the wooing note." " Go back to your wooing days," he said; " think of all the little devices — all of them legitimate — employed in order to woo the affections of the one you loved. Think too, of the little tendernesses paid, and the kindly abounding services rendered when even the flickering response seemed to be a repulse. How you multiplied your attentions and nursed the gracious awakening! Every great preacher is a wooer. . . . We need to woo our people. Let us speak a little more tenderly. Let us drop out the thunder and put in the constraint, and where the thunder has failed the lover may succeed. Not only in the Old Testament but right through the Bible, you will find this wooing and constraining note. Months ago I determined that there should be more of the tender lover in my pulpit spirit, more of the wooing note of the Apostle Paul, more of the gentleness and tender constraint of my Lord." [3] The electric force of this sympathy breaks down every barrier and the souls of preacher and hearer mingle in a common medium of thought and feeling.

[3] *Apostolic Optimism*, pp. 273, 274.

VIII

QUALITIES OF AN EFFECTIVE SERMON

As we set about the work of writing a sermon what are the qualities which we should aim at imparting to it? In other words, what are the questions which will bring our message with carrying and impressive power?

1. The Sermon Must Be a Unified Whole

Unless we can see our subject as an organized, coherent product we are bound to be weakened by confusion and obscurity. The mind instinctively craves for unity. Not only from an artistic point of view is a sermon to be condemned which deals with diverse subjects and ideas: but what is more important — such a sermon defeats the purpose of its production which is to make an impression upon the mind with a view to moving the will. But the mind cannot be impressed nor the will moved by a number of ideas put down side by side, each claiming attention but without an inner link of connection, and therefore with-

out the strength which unity alone bestows. It
has been well said that a good sermon should be
like a wedge — all tending to a point. Yet
" unity is not sameness," as Dr. A. S. Hoyt remarks: " It is consistent with great variety and
even contrast of truths. Diverse and opposite
truths may even enhance the effect of unity, if
there is singleness of ideas underlying all." A
very good plan whereby to make sure that your
sermon is a unity is to give it a title when it is
finished. If after you have done your best to
compose an adequate title, there still remains elements of the sermon which refuse to accept the
label, you may assume that there is present some
material which has no right to be there. Perhaps
the two men who excel all others in the power
thus to provide fitting and striking titles for their
sermons are Cardinal Newman and John Watson.
Here are a few specimens of Watson's skill in
this element of sermonic technique: " Worldliness a Frame of Mind "; " Reasonableness the
Touchstone of Truth "; " Character the Spring of
Life "; " The Power of Other Worldliness ";
These titles are concise, neat, fit their respective
sermons as a glove fits the hand. They are also
suggestive and awaken curiosity.. Dr. Alexander
Whyte says that the very titles of Newman's sermons are a study in homiletics. " To read and
ponder his titles is a stimulus." Consider these

examples the first of which is taken from his *Discourses to Mixed Congregations*, the others from his *Parochial Sermons:* " Saintliness, the Standard of Christian Principle "; " In the World but not of the World "; " Secrecy and Suddenness of Divine Visitations "; " The Cross of Christ, the Measure of the World "; " The Thought of God the Stay of the Soul "; " The Parting of Friends."

2. The Sermon Must Convey the Accent of Conviction

Preach only what you believe, what you have experienced or what you desire to experience. Only those truths which have entered into the very blood and tissue of your being, which have stirred the depths of your own soul, will ring true and have an inspiring effect upon your audience. Decline to preach any doctrines which tradition and authority assert to be true but which are not alive for you. You cannot hope to make them live for other people. As Henry Smith, the Puritan divine puts it: " Let every preacher first see how his notes do move himself, and then he shall have comfort to deliver them to others like an experienced medicine which himself hath proved." [1]   Behind the craving for authority in

[1] Quoted by J. Parker: *Ad Clerum*, p. 49.

religion which so many people feel today, there
is a sound and noble reason. We live in an age
whose most sacred traditions have been challenged.
We know not what a day may bring forth, hence
we pride ourselves on holding our opinions tenta-
tively. As the solid earth beneath our feet has
been dissolved into whirling electrical vortices
so the inner world of the soul threatens to dis-
integrate, and disappear. The cry of today is
for a solid rock on which men can take their stand
and defy the corrosions of doubt and fear. That
rock is built out of religious experience. Do you
believe in God, not as an inference from facts
faithfully gathered from the world without and
open to more than one interpretation, but because
in some moment of insight He rose upon your
soul in tenderness and majesty unspeakable? Such
a conviction will thrill your hearers, and God will
no longer seem to them afar off but nigh at hand
and supremely to be desired. Never forget that
you stand in the pulpit as a witness, and the soul
of your testimony is a conviction born of experience.

3. The Sermon Should Contain an Exposition
of Religious Ideas

We owe it to those who hear us, to many who
are at sea in matters of faith yet also desire some

basis on which to erect a working theory of life,
that we should bring to bear upon the vital questions of our time the knowledge and the patience
of a scholarly intellect.   Mr. John Spargo, the
well-known writer and lecturer on Socialism permits me to quote from a private letter his remark
about his experience as a hearer of sermons: " If
you really want to know what preaching has become, get the reports that appear in the various
newspapers up and down the land, and see what
wretched sophomoric essays are weekly dished up
to adults."   We suffer from a reaction against what
is called doctrinal preaching.   It may be doubtful whether such doctrinal enthusiasts as Canon
Liddon and Dr. R. W. Dale would receive today
the welcome which they enjoyed in their own time.
Yet it remains true that more than ever the world
needs thinkers in the pulpit, men of consecrated
brain who " think through " their message and
know how to express it clearly and realistically.

On investigation you will find that all the great
preachers built their experiences upon a solid
substructure of thought.   Chalmers, Bushnell,
Brooks, Beecher, Channing, Martineau, believed
in the power of ideas, but they took care to present
them steeped in the realities of life and experience.
Read therefore, and not only read but inwardly
digest some of the great masterpieces of religious
genius which are marked by creative and sug-

gestive power such as Schleiermacher's *Discourses on Religion* or Coleridge's *Aids to Reflection*, or Maurice's *Kingdom of Christ*. By such study the mind is furnished with architectonic conceptions and one's preaching takes on dignity and weight. But be careful to eschew all technical terms, the jargon of the class-room. Use language which the average man can understand. You will be agreeably astonished at the response which even uneducated hearers will give to thoughtful discourses, if we take the necessary pains to make them intelligible. Avoid the cold, hard dogmatic method of presentation. F. W. Robertson wrote once to a friend: " Unquestionably the belief in the Divinity of Christ is waning amongst us. They who hold it have petrified it into a theological dogma without life or warmth and thoughtful men are beginning more and more to put it aside." These words are still true. In so far as the pulpit presents theology in a scholastic and academic way, proclaiming its truths in an analytical rather than in a synthetic and concrete fashion, so far is it responsible for the present reaction against theological thinking. What theology has to fear is not clear and masculine thinking, not scientific investigation and laborious painful inquiry but rather unreasoned prejudices, unproved assumptions, traditional assertions which refuse to answer the challenge of open discussion.

A fearless pulpit prepared to follow the argument whithersoever it may lead — this is the crying need of our time. Nor can we forget that the popular magazine is becoming more and more a pulpit from which religion is discussed and a pulpit to which millions who rarely enter a church are listening with keen appreciation. Surely we ought to know at least as much about theology as Mr. H. G. Wells and Sir Oliver Lodge. Be on your guard against the sham sermon in which the preacher undertakes to give a short and easy answer to questions which he has never explored — greatly to the grief of his judicious hearers. A writer in the *Spectator* has remarked that the waning influence of the pulpit is to be traced in part to its relatively low culture. All our congregations contain persons superior to the preacher in almost all spheres of knowledge. Let him see to it that at least in one realm he is master. Of exhortation, of emphasis on the obvious we have more than enough. The ministry of the future must be a teaching ministry. Here as elsewhere there must be a return to Jesus whose most distinctive title was "Teacher." He not only heralded the coming of the kingdom; he explained its laws and set forth its principles. There are men who speak in His name and you might listen to them for years without ever learning what Christianity really is, the real purpose of Jesus, the meaning of Church and prayer. Here is where a vital reform of pulpit method is called for if the spiritual necessities of the hour are to be met.

4. The Sermon Should be Characterized by Clarity of Thought and Expression

We must see the truth clearly before we can hope to make others see it. It is fatal to give the impression that we are groping after something that seems to defy our power of apprehension. Think as carefully and as accurately as the subject you are discussing admits of. One of the ways by which we may gain clearness is to put a statement, about the intelligibility of which we are in doubt, in other and simpler words. The judicious use of repetition and illustration will be found helpful. Clearness of thought and expression is especially necessary in the pulpit, for as the sermon is to be heard, it must be understood at once by the hearer or lost altogether. Principal John Caird, himself a preacher of great distinction, advises the public speaker " to present his thought in varied language or in diversified aspects, to make use of poetical forms and standards and familiar illustrations, to go at a slow pace in argument, to avoid rapid transitions and elliptical reasoning, to be not over-scrupulous as to grammatical and dialectic proprieties or telling roughnesses that jar on a fastidious ear." [2]

Then it is well to bear in mind that the writer of a sermon should recall the mental capacity and the educational status of the congregation for which it is intended. If called upon to address a University audience you would use a style which would be out of place in addressing the villagers of a small country church or the inhabitants of a mining town. But the style should be characterized by perspicuity which, as the grammarians say, implies simplicity, brevity and precision. Much preaching is ruined by the use of inflated or pedantic language, by ambiguous expressions, and by wearisome difficult explanations in which the hearer loses himself and can no longer attend. A recent writer suggests that all ministers should read philosophy, as handled by any of the great masters in order to win the gift of mental clarification. Only, he wisely adds, be careful to keep philosophy out of the sermon where it is an alien and an offence.

5. The Sermon Should Be Constructed in Obedience to Principles of Art

I hold that preaching is a fine art analogous to sculpture, to poetry, to music; and that it is the

[2] *University Addresses*, p. 342.

most exacting of them is abundantly proved by the singular scarceness of those who excel in it. One of the reasons for this paucity of adepts may well be the widespread opinion among preachers that the sermon is a purely utilitarian product with which beauty has nothing whatever to do. And this notion in turn springs, it would seem, from a confusion of thought. It is true that pure art serves no end beyond that of aesthetic satisfaction in the contemplation of beauty, and in this sense art is foreign to the work of constructing sermons. But it is also true that a work serving first and foremost a practical end may yet be so constructed, so aesthetically satisfying, that it is at once a useful object and a thing of beauty, a joy forever. The primary purpose of a Church is to be a meeting-place for an assembly of worshipers. Shall we then forbid the artist to carve his loveliest designs upon the walls or to depict the face of saint and seer upon the windows?

But there is a deeper reason why, if the pulpit is to regain its waning power, it must aim to greater beauty of form. Preaching, to be sure, is much more than an art. It does not exist for its own sake alone, but for the sake of persuading the mind, touching the emotions with the ultimate end of affecting the will. Still the instrument by which these things are done is language, and language has a vital relation to thought, and thought that is beautiful has a tendency to clothe itself in beautiful words. Well has it been said that He whom men called the Word of God came amongst us full not only of the truth that illumines but of the grace that charms. Hence, I agree with the remark of Mahaffy that if by the subtlest logic, by the most deliberate emotion, a man can force his own deepest convictions upon his hearers, then such artistic rhetoric is not only defensible but strongly to be encouraged. In a letter from a private correspondent, a thoughtful layman, a significant criticism touches this point. " The preacher," he writes, " should confine himself closely to his subject. Let him prepare his sermon as a lawyer writes his brief, everything he sets down tending to throw light on the matter in hand. He should avoid being wordy, discursive, and uselessly repetitious. In a game of chess every move should count. If a player moves simply for the sake of making a move, he is apt to be in a bad way, and the game is about up with him. So a preacher should not say anything simply for the sake of saying something." My correspondent, all unwittingly, was laying down an important canon of sound oratory. To avoid mannerisms, tediousness, slipshod and negligent speech, sounding but empty phrases, lame and impotent conclusions, is a work to be achieved only by a devoted and painstaking artist.   Other things being equal, that sermon will best achieve its purpose and evoke a deep response from him who hears it, which is organic, proportioned in structure, impressive by its form and diction, noble and dignified in its ornate harmony.

6. The Style of the Sermon Should Have the Quality of Movement and Progress

" Movement in style," says Vinet, " consists in transferring the hearer from one moral plane or situation to another. This movement is not life but it is the effect and evidence of life. We cannot conceive of life without movement." A static sermon is a dead sermon. It is not enough that the sermon should reflect spiritual truth; it must do more; it must show that truth alive otherwise it will not lay hold of the hearer. One way of gaining this power to vitalize truth is to cultivate the art of varying your thought, of seeing the scenes which form the subjects of your preaching. Some who heard Beecher report that one of the great charms of his oratory was due to constant variation in subject and manner. " He never tired his audience. He would denounce a great evil with tremendous force and power, then tell an amusing story which would move his hearers to laughter; then describe a scene of suffering and distress so dramatically, as to bring tears to the eyes of his listeners, and a moment later would launch an attack upon the oppressors of the poor and needy." [3]   But variety of mood is not enough. The movement must be one of progress.   Every true sermon has an aim to accomplish, a goal to be won.   The psychological order may be movement from the exposition of theory to the duty of practice, it may be from the divine authority of the truth expounded to the necessity of faith on the part of the hearer, or it may be movement in the opposite direction from acceptance of the truth to renewal of life and conduct in this world, and participation in the glory to be revealed in the world to come.   When the sermon is finished you will do well to read it over carefully and discover whether the goal you have set before you has been really reached.   If you have not gained the goal legitimately but have taken a flying leap to it, leaving a yawning chasm of illogicality into which your hearer tumbles, it is obvious that something has gone wrong with the sequence of your thought.   Or if you have simply stopped short and failed to reach the predetermined end, the sermon must be equally condemned, and you must retrace your steps and construct a new order.

[3] Powers: *Portraits of a Half Century*, p. 116.

7. The Sermon Should Keep Close to the Realities of Life

Thoughtful churchgoers complain that they seldom carry away with them any thought that might enable them to understand themselves and to help them in the practical business of living. There are not a few pulpits which have won a reputation for brilliancy, yet their utterances, when analyzed, consist of little more than glittering generalities of " the fatherhood of God," or " the brotherhood of man " variety. But as the flippant Frenchwoman said: " Fine words forsooth! A little cake and wine were more to the point! " In these days men and women demand, as they have never demanded before, that their religious or ethical leaders shall address themselves to the actual, pressing needs of life which must be lived in a world full of danger to any noble faith or spiritual character. Perhaps the greatest weakness of the modern pulpit lies in its failure to bring religious ideas to bear effectually upon life. The preacher often fobs off his hearers with assertions too big to be denied, yet too remote from the practicalities of the hour to be of the slightest help to anybody. And he is encouraged in his aberrations by a certain type of " half-baked " hearer who loves to lose himself in the vague transcendentalism of a sentimental theology.

While the preacher is uttering his *ore rotundo* pronouncements, there sit facing him the business man, the city official, the physician, the lawyer, the banker, the teacher, the newspaper editor, each of them with his problems that baffle and perplex, each of them wistfully looking for some light to illumine his way, some strength to help him bear his burdens and achieve his tasks.

What *does* the average preacher know about the peculiar perplexities of these people? Take the man of business who is engaged in a hand-to-hand fight for a livelihood. How is the preacher who is ignorant of his perplexities, of the temptations which beset him, to say the word that shall help him in the struggle to save his soul alive? There is but one solution of the difficulty. Seminaries can do but little here; the true teacher is experience. The preacher must betimes leave his books, get to know men not simply at the social gathering, but in private heart-to-heart sympathetic intercourse. He must breathe the atmosphere of the office or the bank before he can hope to deal effectively with the moral and spiritual problems of the financier or the man of affairs.

Then, again, the temperament of the preacher is such that he is liable to be so absorbed in the ideal aspects of truth as to neglect the scientific and practical means by which the truth may be realized. Modern-minded persons find law ruling everywhere in the natural order. They suspect that it rules also in the spiritual order. What they want to know is: What are those spiritual laws, and how may they be utilized for the enrichment and expansion of life? It is not enough to glorify the face of goodness. Men must be taught the methods by which they can make goodness their own. The pulpit that is to command the respect of the world today, must be rich in suggestiveness, in scientific aim, in hints that make for practice.

IX

THE DELIVERY OF THE SERMON

LET us suppose that the sermon is completed, but it is only half done: it has to be delivered. So important is this part of preaching that if the delivery be good a mediocre sermon will frequently make an excellent impression whereas a brilliant discourse, if badly delivered, will fall flat. Some young preachers of an ultra-intellectual cast profess a lofty indifference to matters of elocution and general pulpit deportment. They are right when they insist that a trained mind well furnished with relevant knowledge is the essential prerequisite of effective pulpit speech. But everybody knows that a man may be master of a subject and yet be quite unable to communicate it to others, he may be an admirable writer but a very poor speaker. Public speaking in any form is an art and to excel in it demands careful training. To possess ideas is one thing; to interpret them, to render them intelligible and dynamic is another and a different thing. Language, voice, gesture, manner — all play their part in the latter process.

And yet it remains true that these are mere instruments to be used by a power infinitely greater. "Delivery," writes Adolphe Monod "has its residence not in the mouth, but in the *sentiment* and the *thought*. It depends less on the voice than on the soul. . . . It is at bottom, the soul of the speaker which addresses the soul of the hearer. The organs of speech, on the one part, and the organs of hearing on the other, are but intermediates between the mind of him who speaks and the mind of him who hears. The more free one makes his communication, the more one forgets the organ; so as to bring out nothing but the soul, the better will be the elocution. Let the soul, the entire soul, with its constant unity, as well as its infinite moments, look through the utterance like the bottom of a stream through perfectly limpid water, so limpid that it seems not to exist. . . . *It is the soul that should speak.*" [1]

Of the many sermons I have heard I have forgotten the great majority; but some I shall never forget, because of some spiritual quality which revealed itself in the delivery. An audience is delighted to hear a speaker who is master

[1] It is not worth while discussing the *memoriter* method, that is of writing out the sermon in full, learning it off by heart, and then reading the sermon in the pulpit as from a kind of mental photograph, instead of from a manuscript. Very few men can practise this method without becoming bad preachers.

of his theme and who does not hesitate or falter or withdraw one phrase to substitute for it another but pours forth freely and spontaneously the stores of a richly furnished mind. Yet so great is the power of the soul that in some instances it has dispensed with the instrumentalities which it usually demands for its greatest effects. Morley Punshon and Thomas Chalmers were men devoid of all the conventional graces of oratory. Their voices were unpleasing and unmusical; their gestures awkward and mechanical; the Scotsman read his manuscript closely, the Englishman's words rushed in an impetuous torrent so that they threatened at times to submerge his hearers and leave them gasping for breath. Yet both held their audiences as under a magic spell, and triumphed over all external deficiencies. Genius, nevertheless, is subject to no law except that of its own creating. We can admire but we may not imitate. There are, however variously modified, but two ways of delivering a sermon.

1. Reading a Carefully Written Manuscript in the Pulpit

It has become the fashion to condemn this method offhand. As a fact, however, some men can preach only in this way, and if it is forbidden them, they must cease to preach. Especially is this true of those who have followed this method for a long period. Some preachers confess that if they were not held in check by the manuscript they might say the wrong thing or run on in intolerable prolixity. Some feel that owing to a poor verbal memory, or some other temperamental defect, extemporaneous preaching would put upon them an unbearable strain. Moreover there is no doubt that it sets the mind free from anxiety and it sets the preacher free from incoherent babbling and running off into bypaths where he and the hearer are often lost. Some of the most popularly effective sermons I have ever heard were read. I think specially of Bishop Henson, Canon Scott Holland, Dean Farrar and Dr. C. H. Parkhurst. And on the other hand one who heard Newman try on more than one occasion to preach extemporaneously characterized his efforts as " deplorable," " rambling," " incoherent " and " wearisome." No one could hear these men without realizing that for them reading was the best and indeed the only method. Nevertheless it is not to be commended to those who can, at whatever cost, do otherwise. For it labors under two serious disadvantages. It creates a wrong psychological atmosphere. The manuscript, as a rule, is a barrier between the personality of the preacher and that of the hearer. There is no room for that play of the subconscious which, as we have seen, is a factor in the highest type of preaching. The other drawback is that it is growing more and more unpopular. Neither in Congress nor on the platform nor in Courts of Justice would a read speech or address be tolerated. I have indeed seen a man deliberately take a manuscript from his pocket and read an after-dinner oration but, if looks had the power to kill, that man's speech would have remained unuttered. Only conservatism and conventionalism keeps this method in a sort of furtive existence. But more and more the laity demand and will insist on having sermons delivered in a way at once informal and unfettered. This last consideration will probably prove so coercive that in a couple of decades a read sermon will seem a survival of a forgotten custom. Take a plebiscite on the matter in an average congregation and you will find that ninety-five per cent will vote for the abolition of the manuscript.

Still, for a small minority reading will remain the only possible method. How are these preachers to gain the advantages of a freer method with as few disadvantages of the manuscript as possible? One good suggestion is that you should go into the pulpit on Saturday night in the empty church and try to preach your sermon, peopling the pews in your imagination. Be so familiar with your sermon that you can find your way through it easily without keeping the face close to the paper. Another excellent piece of advice is that given by Professor Pattison. " Spare no pains," he says, " to make yourself a good reader. It by no means follows that should you read your sermons your hearers will not detect the lack of oratorical temperament and the presence of natural timidity. Attend to your voice, to its tone and flexibility and emphasis. Charles Dickens learned all his public readings by heart, and knew every word of them without needing to look at the open book which lay on the desk before him. Yet in the anticipation of an engagement he says that he read over the selections often twice a day " with exactly the same pains as at night." [2] When writing the sermon carefully listen to the words as you utter them aloud; and at the same time picture to yourself an audience invisibly present. Put down the sentences in the free unaffected way you would speak them to a friend. By this means naturalness and vitality will be infused into your thought and its expression. You will gain something of the impromptu manner, the quick nervous movement which holds and thrills your audience.

2. The Alternative Method is " Free Delivery "

The one element common to both is the writing of the sermon. All experts are agreed that for

[2] *The Making of the Sermon*, p. 315.

the first five or six years of a preacher's career it is absolutely necessary for him to write out fully his sermons, whichever method he may adopt. Then from the manuscript a careful and logical outline ought to be prepared. The truths set forth ought to possess the preacher's mind, stir his emotions and kindle his imagination. Then he may or may not take the outline into the pulpit. Some feel that even the scantiest notes act as a deterrent not as a help when the moment for pulpit utterance has come. If the outline is used in the pulpit the main headings should be clearly marked so that the eye can easily catch them.

Free delivery means strenuous preparation with pen in hand. It means hard work in which intellect, emotions, imagination and will have a share. "All the great speakers," says Archbishop Magee, "write and write constantly. Only thus can you acquire accuracy, force, terseness. Never give up the habit of writing." With scarcely an exception men who have attained distinction in the art of extempore speaking have in their earlier years written out their discourses; and it will be found that even in their later years when practice in delivery made this work easier they did not wholly abandon the pen.

There are great advantages in this method which commend it as the goal toward which the student should bend his energies.

1. It enables y.ou to get *en rapport* with your audience. Your presence in the pulpit with a sermon in which you have confidence firmly fixed in your mind, and the presence of a congregation prepared to listen are simply the necessary conditions for the act of preaching. Before preaching takes place the preacher and the hearer must have a spiritual bond between them. This is best accomplished when the speaker allows nothing to come between him and his auditors, but stands erect and speaks to them out of a full mind in the simplest and directest manner possible. The nearer you get to your hearers the more telling will be your utterance.

2. This method allows you to take advantage of those thoughts and images flung out in the heat of preaching. The mind is working at high pressure. Ideas and similes stored up in the subconscious break through into consciousness, strengthening the flow of thought and adding to the imaginative power of the sermon as a whole.

3. It is oratorically effective. Free speech is the highest form of eloquence. Fenelon says that the orations of Demosthenes and Cicero give evidence that they were not committed to memory word for word. For example, Cicero speaks at times sentences adapted to incidents which happened at the moment, and which could not possibly, therefore, have been prepared previously. It

is true that you will not, by this method, be always at your best. What of it? You will compensate for this at other times by the freedom and ease of your utterance, the vigorous handling of your thought, and the impassioned quality of your words. You will grow in effectiveness. Your message will have the note of reality generally absent from read discourse.

Doubtless this method is the most difficult to acquire. Doubtless, also, you will forget at times some particularly fine sentence which you wished to remember, or you may begin a sentence not knowing how to finish it, and you may pause, not rhetorically, but in an agony of perplexity, wondering what will happen next. The finish of your language may leave something to be desired. But what you lose in these ways you gain in others, notably in freedom and in driving power. This last point I would emphasize. Many sermons contain sound ideas clothed in picturesque, lucid English, but fail in spite of these virtues because they lack the impact of the will, the urge of the preacher's personality released upon his hearers. It is this mobile force which projects the truth into their minds. Since the war there is an insistent demand for greater reality in all the relationships of life. Hence men value direct and robust speaking and consider *what* you say more than *how* you say it. This is what lies at the bottom of the

demand so often heard for " straight from the
shoulder " talks. Here is the secret of the success
of such religious teachers as Mr. Studdert Ken-
nedy and Miss Maude Royden. The true ideal of
preaching is that which combines form and matter,
thought and expression, the whole fired into the
glow and vitality of a passionate conviction.

Now let me suppose that you have entered the
pulpit, and are about to deliver your message. It
it the custom in some churches to preface the
sermon with a brief prayer. Unhappily this
prayer is frequently pronounced in a perfunctory
and half-audible tone and the congregation gets
the impression that it is a seemly convention without any special significance. Obviously the real
value of such a prayer is to create the devotional
mood, the sense of the Divine presence which is
the very soul of religion. Let the prayer be
omitted, if you will, on the ground that the preceding acts of worship render it unnecessary; or if
you prefer to follow the ordinary usage, take
particular pains that the prayer should be worded
and uttered with clearness, reverence and relevance.

As you face your audience what are the qualities
of your delivery which will render it effective?

1. *Simplicity*. One might suppose that this
virtue of all virtues in public speaking is the easiest
to practice; in reality it is the hardest. There is

an ingrained tendency, the result of inherited teaching, in many preachers to assume, once they have entered the pulpit, a special pose, a different tone, and a type of language identified with the situation. A generation ago the prevailing type of pulpit speech was declamatory, and in the best sense " oratorical." The great preachers of that time won their success not by virtue of but in spite of their rhetorical artifices. The bad legacy which they have left us is seen in that preachiness of tone into which the best of pulpit speakers occasionally fall. Yet today nothing is more hurtful to genuine utterances. What the hearer demands is simple, natural and at times impassioned quality of speech. And to achieve this the speaker must constantly remind himself that the norm of all effective preaching is a variant on the conversational style. " Oratory is expanded conversation, the extension of the range of voice as found in everyday speech. When faults occur in the delivery of the sermon, there is some departure from the elemental modulations of conversation. Any man with a tendency to drift can correct this fault in a measure by addressing men in a direct and simple way, enlarging for his congregation the natural method employed in speaking tone." [3]

There is, however, a danger to be guarded against. Churches are not always built in order

[3] Curry: *Vocal and Literary Interpretation of the Bible*, p. 6.

that speech may be heard in them, hence the preacher must rise above his conversational tone that all may catch what he has to say. In doing so, however, he is liable to change the quality of his tone. An element of pseudo-rhetoric enters into it and the fundamental law of simplicity is violated. When this happens and the preacher is conscious of it, the wise course is to pause for a moment and deliberately change the register of his voice. It is a curious fact that the pulpit it-self has on some men a bad effect. Let them stand anywhere else in the Church and they are simple and natural; in the pulpit their speech becomes inflated and pompous and labored — an-other illustration of the power of suggestion. Practice of the art of natural speaking in the pulpit in the presence of a few critical friends will cure this fault. No pains can be too great, no work too arduous if only the result is the winning of the grace of simplicity. A recent writer relates his experience when he heard a far-famed pulpit orator. " A large congregation greeted him. I fancy that the majority of them, like myself, expected to be thrilled by his eloquence. We were thrilled but not just in the manner we expected. At all times during the progress of the sermon, his delivery was simple, intimate, intense, con-versational. ' But,' you would ask, ' was it effec-tive? ' Extremely so. It was animated and arresting, and being so, it attracted and held the attention. I remember very distinctly that, at the conclusion of the sermon I thought, what a short sermon! To my surprise, upon looking at my watch, I found that he had spoken for an hour." Simplicity implies sincerity. A man may be himself sincere yet he may, through bad example or wrong teaching, have an insincere delivery. The truth we are commissioned to proclaim is too lofty, the interests at stake too tremendous to tolerate for a moment the slightest mixture of unreality or artificiality in our mode of utterance. It is the accent of sincerity that opens a path for your word to the heart and conscience of your hearer. "I never heard Joseph Parker," said the late W. Robertson Nicoll, "without wanting to be a better man." No nobler tribute can be paid to any preacher and only he can earn it who seeks for no effect save that which a true and sincere soul produces upon other souls.

2. *Self-possession.* Simplicity and naturalness of delivery are impossible apart from self-possession, freedom of mind. The enemy of self-possession is, of course, self-consciousness, which rises at times into a paralyzing dread. Some of the greatest orators and preachers have confessed to feelings of nervousness and timidity immediately before rising up to speak. Phillips Brooks

told a friend that he never spoke in public without being intensely nervous. Boyd Carpenter said to his daughter that his nervousness was so great that often when he arrived in the pulpit he could remember nothing of what he was going to say and that he only knew where the text was, but that after giving that out gradually the subject would begin to unroll itself. Even such a manly and self-reliant character as Norman Macleod wrote to his wife that when preaching before royalty at Balmoral he had to make an effort to " forget the great ones I saw and to remember the great Ones I saw not," adding, " I preached from my heart and with as much freedom as at a mission station." These testimonies suggest that a nervous condition may be a help rather than a hindrance to a speaker. Indeed it may be doubted if a sermon can communicate itself to the hearer and lay hold of him, in the absence of some nervous tension on the part of the preacher. Only this nervousness must be kept firmly under control. F. W. Robertson preached always in a state of great excitement, but this excitement was so controlled that instead of interfering with the flow of thought, or freedom in delivery, it hastened the one and imparted to the other a thrilling power which made him a great " master of assemblies."

Samuel Wilberforce, the most eloquent bishop

of his time admitted that his nervousness in the pulpit was so great that he required to have " something before him, were it only a bundle of blank paper." Charles Kingsley said that when preaching in Westminster Abbey, he wished as he walked to the pulpit that he were dead, and that when he stood in it he wished he were deader! There is the sensitiveness which goes with the oratorical temperament. The man of phlegmatic disposition will never make an effectve public speaker. If therefore, you are mentally agitated as you are about to deliver your discourse, reflect that this is the condition of success and be thankful. Only do not allow yourself to lose self-control; take a few deep breaths and begin slowly and with much deliberation. As the cause of pulpit-fright is self-consciousness, its cure must be concentration on something else. The Abbé Bautain relates a remarkable experience which befell him and which teaches a lesson much needed by many a preacher. " One day," he writes, " I had to preach in one of the principal churches in Paris. There was an immense audience. As I was ascending the pulpit, I perceived a person whom I had supposed absent, and my mind was carried away suddenly by a train of recollections. I reached the pulpit-landing, knelt down as usual and when I should have risen to speak, I had forgotten not only my text but even the subject of

my sermon. . . . My embarrassment and an-
guish may be conceived. Nevertheless not losing
head or heart I looked full at my danger without
being scared by it, yet without seeing how I was
to get out of it. At last I had recourse to God and
I said to Him from the very bottom of my heart
and with all the fervor of my anxiety — ' Lord,
if it be Thy will that I preach, give me back my
plan '; and at that instant, my text came back to
my mind, and with my text the subject. I think
that never in my life have I experienced anything
more astonishing, nor a more lively emotion of
gratitude." [4] The small occasion of the good
Abbé's perturbation is typical of many. Fear of
failure to make an impression on the audience,
fear of someone in the congregation more learned
or more eloquent than the preacher, fear of dis-
pleasing somebody present, fear of forgetfulness,
fear of saying something irritating to the less open-
minded hearers, fear of being afraid, fear because
of a general predisposition of being afraid of anything that presents itself as a duty, fear because of
imperfect preparation — such are some but only
some of the demons that haunt the pulpit. How
are they to be exorcised?

To begin with, each victim must find out for
himself his own particular enemy. Examine it
thoroughly, see it in its real nature as most fre-

[4] *Op. cit.*, pp. 258, 259.

quently the product of a morbid imagination. For example, the fear of forgetfulness is overcome by reflecting that the more you trust your memory the more it will answer your trust. The fear of failure cannot hold out against this solid principle — *you can do what you think you can do.* If you think that you cannot preach with ease and freedom, your failure is foreordained — by yourself. Are you afraid of this or that individual? Turn the mind from him and concentrate it on others before you who, you have reason to believe, are happy to be present and await your message with agreeable anticipation. There is however, a demoniacal fear which ought to vex you if you enter the pulpit unprepared. "Perfect preparation casteth out fear." Fill your mind with your subject. Breathe its atmosphere. Be master of its outs and ins. As the psalmist could say, "I am prayer," [5] be it yours to say, "I am the sermon." This concentration on your theme filling the entire field of consciousness will exclude any distressing preoccupation with yourself. As you speak, concentrate all your energies on gaining and holding the attention of the audience to the ideas you are expressing. In brief, cease to think about yourself by being absorbed in your theme and in a forcible, virile, attractive presentation of it.

[5] Psalm CIX, 4 (literal rendering of the Hebrew).

3. *Variety*. Monotony whether in thought or in expression kills all interest because it annoys and repels the hearer. This is why nerve specialists recommend patients suffering from insomnia to attend some churches where the congregation is lulled to sleep under the unvarying tones issuing from the pulpit. Monotony of thought must be met and overcome by variety of thought. As we think we pass from one point of view or mental situation to another. To realize vividly each changing thought, to let the mind's creative activity have full scope is to achieve variety of ideas. The mind is the best example of diversity in unity. " If there are no two leaves on a tree exactly alike, still less are there two sentiments in a human soul which are perfectly identical." Therefore be true to each thought as it emerges in consciousness, and your delivery will take on vivacity and impressiveness. Some thoughts must be expressed slowly with pause and emphasis, other thoughts ask to be uttered quickly yet not so quickly as to dull clearness of enunciation.

If, as has been emphasized, preaching is elevated conversation, one of the best ways for gaining the variety and liveliness essential to the art is to study conversation carefully. Listen to several people conversing together and mark how agile the human voice is as it reflects the ever varying movement, the subtle change of feeling, the peculiar hues of mind, the delicate shades of imagination, all of which make the never-dying charm of conversation. Now this is what we want to hear from the pulpit, and wherever it is heard the empty pews are few and far between. The preacher therefore, before entering the pulpit should remind himself that he is not about to deliver an oration but to conduct a conversation on a religious subject. Should he find himself drifting away from this attitude, he should pause for a moment, and re-assume the conversational tone. It is fatal to seek variety by raising the voice and shouting. The effect is to alienate the hearer and cause him to desire that you should make an end as speedily as possible. It is, I believe, a fact that the preacher often raises his voice when his ideas have given out, as if to make up for the paucity of thought by sheer physical energy. Fenelon tells that on one occasion he fell asleep at an afternoon sermon. " I soon awakened and I heard the preacher throwing himself into an extraordinary state of excitement, so that for a moment I supposed that he was discussing some extremely important ethical question. . . . He was only giving notice to his hearers that on the following Sunday he would preach on penitence. . . . I would have laughed had not respect for the place and the service forbidden it." [6] Realize

[6] *Dialogues on Eloquence* (2nd Dial.).

definitely each idea and the suitable expression of it will, if the mind is free, come spontaneously to the lips. And with this realization must go truthfulness of feeling. We must study the impression which the thought has made on our own minds, and this impression will lead to the right expression. We shall not fall into the error of infusing into our utterances a greater warmth than we feel or than the idea calls for, nor shall we announce majestic truths in cold and unimpassioned tones.

So far we have been thinking about the moral elements in delivery; a few words about the physical elements may be added. If we were disembodied spirits, doubtless thought well conceived would automatically communicate itself and make its fit impression. But we utter what is within by means of a physical organism, that is to say, by voice, gesture and look. There is no gift which a preacher might so much covet as the gift of a rich and copious voice. There are few perfect voices; it will be found that nearly every voice lacks this or that quality. Experience proves, however, that this lack can be atoned for by the presence in an abundant manner of other characteristics. The voice of Chalmers was thick and guttural but it was powerful and by sheer energy, begotten of spiritual zeal, bore down all before it. Newman's voice was exquisitely musical but utterly, wanting in oratorical power. Whatever type of voice you have, make the most of it by careful training under a competent teacher. The vocal faults of the preacher spring from failure to let the vocal cords have free play and from the wrong use of the voice and throat in speaking. There are a few qualities which are absolutely essential to effective delivery and these should be acquired at whatever cost of time and labor.

1. *Clearness of enunciation.* All speech is produced by the utterance of open tones called vowels and by certain utterances called consonants. Clear enunciation is attained by practicing the clear utterance of every syllable. This clearness of tone will make up for weakness in the volume of the voice. When every syllable gets its full value, with special attention to the last syllable of a sentence, the sermon is heard from the text to the last word. It was this power to syllabize which was no small factor in the dramatic and compelling quality of Joseph Parker's delivery. Men and women often went to hear him simply to get lessons in the art of speaking. Voice culturists have a saying well worth remembering. "Take care of the consonants and the vowels will take care of themselves."

2. *Variations of tone.* Nothing is more wearisome than a persistently loud tone in preaching. It has a tendency to deafen and confuse the

hearer; the voice ceases to be a subsidiary agent and occupies too much of the attention. John Bright said of a speaker who had voice and nothing else, — " He speaks extremely well, if you do not listen to what he says." On the other hand, a voice pitched on too low a key wearies the hearer by the demand it makes for the effort to listen. It is sad to see on some faces a grim determination that come what will the owners *will* listen. The safe rule is to discover the compass of your voice; if you speak outside it, you become strident and guttural. Strike for the middle note as the basis of your utterance. You can rise above it or fall below it in correspondence with the changing actions of the mind.

3. *Carrying power.* If you produce the tones properly your voice will carry to the limits of any church building. But the correct tone production is impossible unless the muscles of the throat are completely released. Any constriction there leads to false notes and a wrong use of the voice. An excellent suggestion for the acquirement of carrying power with a conversational tone is to take the finished sermon and while seated repeat it as in ordinary conversation, paragraph by paragraph, to a friend seated near you. After the first paragraph place your friend a little farther away, continue in conversational tone the succeeding paragraph, taking care to accentuate sponta-

neously whenever accentuation is necessary. Continue this exercise until you are satisfied and your long-suffering friend is satisfied that you can deliver the sermon with raised voice yet without deserting the conversational tone. Again let it be said, preaching is enlarged conversation. It is the speaker conversing with a large number of persons instead of a single individual.

The most effective delivery uses the entire body as its instrument. Gesture has its place in communicating your message, only unhappily, it is too often out of its place. Its law is also the law of naturalness and simplicity. Sometimes it becomes a mere mannerism which means nothing and therefore conveys nothing. There is a distinguished American preacher whose sermon is accompanied by a continuous see-sawing movement of his right arm while the other remains stiffly by his side. At first you are annoyed but after a little you ignore it because of the value and interest of what the speaker has to say. But why waste so much energy? Far better to eliminate such meaningless motions. Reserve of gestures is to be commended. They will be appreciated when they do come to heighten the emphasis on the significant and telling passages because they will then be spontaneous and in harmony with the situation. Any suspicion of artificiality or of a pre-arranged harmony between word and action, savoring as it does of unreality, spells its own condemnation. "The devil of unreality goes about like a roaring lion seeking whom he may devour. If he is allowed to get in and make himself at home among your habits of speech and of life he will eat you up almost before you know it." David Garrick was once asked by a young clergyman for advice as to his deportment in the pulpit. The great actor gave him wise counsel. "You know how you would speak in the parlor to a dear friend who was in imminent danger of his life. . . . You would not think of playing the orator. You would be yourself; and the interesting nature of your subject, impressing your heart, would furnish you with the most natural tone of voice, the most proper language, the most engaging pictures, and the most suitable and graceful gestures. What you would be in the parlor, be in the pulpit; and you will not fail to please, to effect, to profit."

And so we come back to the moral and spiritual background of the preacher's own soul where the secret dwells. Have you a deep sympathy with the woe and tragedy of human life? As you look into the faces of men and women before you do you try to realize that each soul leads a very lonely life, yet yearns for some kindred spirit to look within and whisper the healing and reconciling word? Have you but one ambition, to say something that may cheer the faint-hearted, console the sorrow-laden, strengthen the tempted, inspire the doubting and bring the peace of God into the hearts of the anxious and the foreboding? Then indeed your message will be with power for on you will fall the mystic gift before which every door of the soul flies open and you enter into the joy of comradeship with man that cleanses and helps and saves.

X

ANALYTICAL STUDY OF THREE SERMONS

THREE sermons which may be found in the Appendix have been selected for study: (1) because of their intrinsic worth; (2) because of their suitability as models for students of the art of sermon construction; (3) because though written by men of very different mental disposition, they illustrate the principles which have been set forth in this book.

The first example is a sermon by Dr. J. H. Jowett on the text: "I have been crucified with Christ; yet I live; and yet no longer I but Christ liveth in me; and that life which I now live in the flesh I live in faith, the faith which is in the Son of God, who loved me and gave himself for me." (Gal. II, 20.) The sermon is taken from a volume entitled, *The Transfigured Church*, (F. H. Revell Company).

PLAN OF SERMON

The Introduction

"What shall I do with this passage? . . . Shall we come to it as guests or as controversialists? . . . I come to feast and not to fight."

Statement of Theme and Divisions

" Behind the familiar words of my text are tremendous experiences." . . . " The passion of redemption." . . . " The mystery of re-creation." . . . " The secret of appropriation."

Working Out of the Theme

A I *The Passion of Redemption:* " The Son of God who loved me and gave himself for me." But at once notice an obtrusion which so many of our modern preachers resent. " Who loved me." " That is neurotic and we prefer the philosophic." And so there are two processes at work. (*a*) " The de-sentimentalizing of the religious life "; (*b*) " Because we de-sentimentalize there is a correlative process, and we de-personalize." (*c*) " Is not all this wrong then and attended by infinite peril? " (*d*) " The personal and the emotional have had their power and ministry in the lives of all conspicuous saints." For example, Paul, Luther, Calvin, Spurgeon.

II " What was the purpose of the Lord's redemption? "   " Humanity lay in a dire and a woeful bondage." . . . " The Lord loved the bondslave." . . . " He loved."

(*a*) " Now love is *holy*." " O give thanks at the remembrance of his holiness! " " Love is holiness in exercise, it is holiness in gracious movement."

(*b*) And because love is holy, love is inconceivably *sensitive*. " The unhallowed is the insensitive." . . . " And therefore it is impossible for us to realize, even remotely, the sensitiveness of holiness, and therefore, again, our Saviour's sorrows are inconceivable." " Was ever sorrow like unto my sorrow? "

(*c*) " And because holy love is sensitive, holy love is *redemptive*." " Holiness is not secretive, exclusive, but sanative and redemptive."

(*d*) " *He gave himself for me*." " For holy, sensitive, redemptive love must of necessity be sacrificial."

B " Now let us pass to the secret of appropriation." " The virtues of the love-sacrifice are to be mine by faith." . . .

" What is faith? " . . . " Faith is the personal dealing with Christ." " Faith is not finally mental or emotional but volitional." . . . " It is the personal surrender of life to the governance of the Saviourhood of Christ." " Faith is the human end of the ministry which establishes union between the soul and its Lord." " Such is the secret of appropriation."

C   *The wonders of re-creation.*

What are to be the issues of the union?

(1) *Mortification.* " I   am   crucified   with

Christ." "One of the gifts of redemption is a certain deadness" . . . "deadness to the threat of yesterday, deadness to the fear of tomorrow, deadness to the power of the immediate circumstance, and deadness to majestic death itself."

(2) *Vitalization.* "Yet I live." "Dormant power shall be aroused and shall troop forth out of their graves." . . . "And old powers shall be renewed."

(3) *The Manifestation of Christ. Yet no Longer I but Christ!* "What is that but the conversion and transfiguration of the ego and the emergence of the Lord?" . . . "The Lord who pervades the life also dominates it." . . . "Yes, that is the Christian ideal, and that is the Christian friendship." . . . "My activities are the motions of my Lord." . . . "Men shall gaze upon the issues of the life and shall say: It is the Lord! And they shall glorify our Father which is in heaven."

The student will observe that the numerals and letters are put in simply to make the analysis clear. They are not in the sermon, and yet the preacher discloses at the beginning the divisions of this theme. Moreover he states his theme. "Behind the familiar words of my text are tremendous experiences, the secrets of which lead us into the innermost sanctuary of the hallowed love and grace of God."

The divisions are not imposed upon the text but naturally spring out of it. Hence we have an admirable example of expository preaching. There is no diffuseness, no wandering from the path marked out in the preacher's thought, no losing sight of his great theme — the " wonders of redemption." Scripture is illustrated by Scripture, and the significance of each element of the text is lucidly exploited. Observe also that the introduction is brief, catches the attention at once by rhetorical questions and the illustration of the fight around the farmhouse at Waterloo. Nothing is in the introduction which more properly should belong to the development of the subject. It is brief, consisting of about one page in a sermon which covers a trifle more than twelve pages in the original text.

Special attention is directed to the conclusion. Here there is no formal application, because the truth proclaimed has been applied throughout the discourse. The sermon has been highly mystical and transcendental throughout: it closes with the note of social service. These high experiences, these wonders of redemption are not to be self-ishly enjoyed; they must inevitably issue in rebuking the Pharisee, denouncing the oppressor, ministering to the hungry, the paralyzed and the fever-stricken and in championing the cause of the Magdalene and the little child — The whole issue is the glory of God the Father. There is movement, progress, the stir of purposive life throughout the sermon. So much for the structure of the discourse. Let us now turn to the style and diction.

We do not read far without seeing that we have here a master of clear, nervous, picturesque style. The thought is beautiful and is clothed in beautiful dress. There are no loose rambling sentences; the language fits the thought as a well made glove fits the hand. Lucidity is also characteristic of Dr. Jowett's manner. The language is a clear glass through which the thought shines brightly. There are many phrases which may be described as " pictographic." Take as examples: " A perfectly dry eye is blind, and a perfectly dry religion has no sight." " Sentimentalism is born among the flowers; a noble sentiment is born among snows." " The powers shall be aroused and shall troop forth out of their graves." Note how inevitably the sermon moves to its appointed goal. No stagnation, no dull patches; the sermon gives the appearance of having been written when the preacher's mind was aglow with heat and life. This sense of energy is achieved by frequent questions and exclamations, by passing quickly from a thought that has been sufficiently expressed to another suggested by way of similarity or of contrast. Note also the appropriateness of the quotations from the Bible. Lastly, the interest of the sermon is sustained throughout by similes, illustrations, and images. The student should make a list of these and mark what proportion of the images is visual and what proportion auditory. He should also try to answer these questions: " What quality or qualities in this discourse make a special impression on me? " " Do my sermons contain these qualities? " Would the preacher have improved the sermon if he had shown Paul's sensitiveness to the non-Christian thought of his day? Compare this sermon with Alexander Maclaren's and Phillips Brooks's treatment of the same text.

The second example, a sermon on " Procrastination " by Dr. Harry Emerson Fosdick, is from *Great Modern Sermons* edited by H. S. McKeehan (F. H. Revell Company). The sermon is based on Acts XXIV, 25; " When I have a convenient season I will call for thee."

The Plan of the Sermon

is obvious and requires only the barest outline.

The Introduction

The preacher opens quite simply with the announcement of his theme — Procrastination — and proceeds at once to draw a picture of Paul's

situation, followed by a brief sketch of the character of Felix. " Felix lost the supreme opportunity
of his life." So do " we make failures of our
lives."

The Divisions

are indicated by a recurring phrase, " pick up the
words of Felix."

A   These words are *full of hope*.   Procrastination is " the abuse of hope"; it blinds our eyes to
the opportunities and privileges we have in our
hands.

B   These words imply that Felix thinks he has
postponed decision whereas in reality he has not.
" Life's processes do not call a halt simply because
we have not made up our minds." Procrastination is irretrievable decision." This principle is
applicable to our relations to the duties of life."

(*a*) Humanitarian causes.   (*b*) Commonplace
duty of honesty.   (*c*) Avoidance of war.   (*d*) The
claim of the Christian life.

C   These words imply that Felix believes there
will be another opportunity but he is mistaken.
" There is such a thing as being too late."   It is
" accentuated by the conspicuous fact of habit,"
and by the fact of death.   The conclusion is an
appeal to accept the faith of Christ.

This sermon is characterized by qualities which
make for popular effectiveness.   Note the *viva-*

city of the sermon produced by the quick transition of thought and the conversational tone sustained throughout. Note also the *timeliness* of the applications of the truths expounded, *e.g.*, the famine in China, the danger of war, and the choice of a profession. Observe the clearness of the thought. There is nothing obscure. Abundant similes and illustrations make doubt as to the preacher's meaning impossible. Finally consider the *ethical tone* of the discourse. It is based on moral principles verified by experience. The student should make a list of the auditory, visual and motor images employed by the preacher. After reading the sermon aloud he should ask himself the following questions: 1. Does this sermon leave me cold or interested and moved? 2. If the former, is the fault in myself or in the sermon? 3. Are the divisions logical? Does A overlap to any degree C? 4. Does the sermon give a sense of movement and progress? 5. Is there sufficient intellectual substance? 6. Is this sermon an illustration of the principle that the highest art is the concealment of art? Justify your opinion by reasons. Is there any quality desirable in a sermon but which is not to be found here? 7. It is suggested that the sermon should end with the words " You would better choose Him now." Justify this opinion on psychological grounds.

There are two mental exercises which the student should perform. He should compare this sermon with one by Liddon on the same text, marking those points in which each discourse proves itself superior to the other. After some weeks have elapsed he should write a sermon himself on the text, and then compare it with the two he has studied.

The third example is a sermon by Dr. Elwood Worcester printed for private circulation. Its title is simply " Religion." It is selected as a sample of the more thoughtful type of American preaching. There are no figures or other devices for marking the stages of thought. The student will also observe that it differs from the two preceding sermons in that it has no introduction in the technical sense. The preacher reads out his text, states at once in a clear and crisp sentence, what he proposes to preach about, and then passes at once to the discussion.

The Plan of the Sermon

The Introduction

The Theme

" What religion means to us and what we mean by religion."

I   Religion a characteristic of human nature.

(*a*) " Religion . . . the most inalienable endowment of the human race. However far back we go, we never are able to go back to a time when religion was not." Religion is as old as humanity. This is the first thought.

(*b*) The second is that religion is found in the lowest representatives of the race. Some religious ideas were and are present in the most darkened minds.

(*c*) Here then is an "amazing" fact, that "religion has endured so long and has triumphed over so many vicissitudes." It has grappled with many enemies but has risen again, "only purified and strengthened."

II Religion comes to perfection in Jesus Christ. The uniqueness of the Christian religion lies in "the clear conception of Jesus" that "life is active service, a ministry of love and compassion, the conquest of evil by good, sacrifice as a saving and helping of men." The religion of Jesus as a redemptive force may be summed up in the phrase, "The Kingdom of God."

III "Prayer is a great element in religion." Here again the preacher recalls the universality of religion, only now it is religion as prayer. He has been speaking of religion in the history of the past, he now views it as a present experience. Prayer is natural to man, for man is a soul. This leads the preacher to consider the mystery of the soul and its survival of death.

Here is the true explanation of religion. Man is in contact with a creative purpose, a living presence, love, truth, beauty, power. " In this search for God if men had found nothing would they have searched so long? . . . To the Lord Jesus the eternal world of power stood open. On this his religion was founded. . . . The yielding of ourselves to this Reality . . . we call prayer."

IV The Permanence of Religion. " Men have discovered divine things in the past." . . . " We have a rich and glorious inheritance from the past, above all in the Bible." . . . " There will never be another Jesus . . . another St. Paul . . . never another sacred book like the Bible." " Nor is it only the dead " who speak to us. All around us are men and women who minister to us in divine things. The sermon closes with reference to the buried bells of the old legend, symbolical of the love and memory, sorrow and hope which rise from the depths of the heart.

The student ought to notice whether the sermon fulfilled what it set out to do. Does it leave the impression that religion is a great and wonderful thing, that it has done great and wonderful things, and can do them again in the individual and society? Then the diction deserves study. Observe that it is fresh, living, picturesque, at times highly symbolical. It is in harmony with the sublimity of the subject discussed. Note the similes and illustrations and especially the visual images.

The student in analyzing this sermon should ask certain critical questions: 1. What relation has the text to the sermon? Is it really a text or only a motto? 2. Would the sermon be improved if the preacher were to indicate more clearly the line along which his thought moves? 3. Before concluding would the preacher have helped the audience to remember his arguments if he had briefly brought out the actual achievement of his purpose as stated at the outset? 4. What are the qualities of power in this sermon? 5. Is there anything here in the thought or mode of expression absent from my own composition which I might well covet? 6. It is suggested that the sermon should end with the words, " likewise from another world." Why? 7. Can I suggest a better title?

APPENDIX

I.

THE WONDERS OF REDEMPTION

" I have been crucified with Christ; yet I live; and yet no longer I, but Christ liveth in me; and that life which I now live in the flesh I live in faith, the faith which is in the Son of God, who loved me, and gave Himself for me." GAL. ii. 20.

WHAT shall we do with this passage? How shall we approach it? Shall we come to it as guests or as controversialists, as suppliants or as combatants? The fiercest action at Waterloo was fought round about a farm, where the fruits were ripening in the orchard, and the fields were mellowing for the harvest. The farmstead was treated as a battlefield, and the plough-shares were beaten into swords, and the pruning hooks were converted into spears, and the blowing corn was trampled in the gory clay. And here, too, is a farmstead, and the fruit hangs ripe upon the branches, and the corn is yellow for the harvest. How then? Shall we make it a sort of Waterloo, or shall we walk with our Lord in the garden " at the cool of the day " ? I would approach it as a guest and not as a soldier. I come to feast and not to fight. I would " sit down under the shadow," and His fruit shall be " sweet unto my taste." Behind the familiar words of my text there are tremendous experiences, the secrets of which lead us into the innermost sanctuary of the hallowed love and grace of God. And therefore I say I would rather sing the song of the harvest-home than the song of any victor whose ecclesiastical enemy lies prone upon the bloody field. Survey the field! "*Who loved me and gave Himself for me.*" There we have the passion of redemption. "*I am crucified with Christ, yet I live.*" There we have the mystery of re-creation. "*I live in faith, the faith which is in the Son of God.*" There we have the secret of appropriation. Such is this Scriptural farmstead in whose overflowing fields and barns it is our privilege to make our home.

Here, then, is *the passion of redemption*. "The Son of God who loved me, and gave Himself for me." But at once notice an obtrusion which so many of our modern thinkers seem to resent. "Who *loved* me." That is neurotic, and we prefer the philosophic. It is sentimental, and we prefer the mental. The light is too glaring, too sensational, to perfervid, too sunny, and we prefer the cooler and less exciting radiance of the moon. "Who *loved* me." The emotions are stealing into the mind, like a moist Alpine mist rising from the vale, and mixing itself with the light of common day, and many moderns resent the combination. They regard the ministry of emotion as deflecting the judgment; they prefer desiccated light, dry light, light which is absolutely proof against the invasion of sentiment and tears.

And so there are two processes at work. First, there is the de-sentimentalising of the religious life. We shy at sentiment as we should shy at known poison. We are loud in proclaiming the perils of an emotional religion, and we are busy draining away the emotion and leaving the religion hard and dry. And because we de-sentimentalise there is a correlative process, and we de-personalise. Personal love is transformed into diffused energy, the ministering angels become established laws, delicate intimacies are regarded as the interaction of psychic forces, the personal pronouns become abstract nouns, the personal movement in the verb becomes a mere current of the cosmos in which the sacredness of individuality is entirely lost. Here is a contrast which I will present to you as indicating this particular peril of our time. On the one hand, " Where two or three are gathered together in My name there am I in the midst of them." And on the other hand, " The psychic forces are ubiquitous and communion is established by pure volition."

Well, is not all this very thin, and attended by infinite peril? We all recognise the dangers of an emotional piety, but there are almost equally great dangers in a piety from which emotion is entirely banished. A perfectly dry eye is blind, and a perfectly dry religion has no sight. We always have the clearest vision when there's moisture in the air, and a wise personal sentiment has its appointed place in the vision of God, and in the creation of a fruitful intercourse between the soul and Him. The personal and the emotional have had their prominent ministry in the lives of all conspicuous saints. It is certainly true of Paul; the sentence in my text is typical of many more. " Who loved me and gave

Himself for me!" "Weigh diligently," says Martin Luther, "every word of Paul, and especially mark well his pronouns . . . wherein also there is ever some vehemency and power." And it is all equally true of Luther himself. Take his great commentary on the Epistle to the Galatians, and you will find that although it is so martial in its mood, and so severely and consistently polemical, yet the personal emphasis is rarely absent, and the emotions are frequently stirred like the brimming fullness of the spring tides. Even Calvin himself becomes emotional, and a tender sentiment lies upon his thought, like the dews upon the open moors, when he contemplates the wonders of redeeming grace. If we have ever been tempted to think of Calvin as hard and dry and rigid, more a herbalist than a gardener, with the scheme of his thought stretching over his life like a rainless sky, a man devoid of sentiment and incapable of tears — if such has been our thought of Calvin, let us accompany him through the Epistle to the Ephesians, and we shall discover how the merely theological becomes the devotional, how the severely controversial becomes the worshipful, how argument breaks into rapture, and how restrained emotion bursts its dykes, and the man's adoration becomes moist with grateful tears. It is all equally true of another man, nearer to our own time, who is not eclipsed even when set in the radiant succession of Calvin and Luther and Paul. There is nothing more characteristic of Spurgeon than the personal emphasis, the daring use of the pronouns, and the rich, full sentiment that ever plays about his contemplations of the grace and love of his Lord. The greatest wonder in the two worlds of heaven and earth he says is this, that " He loved me, and gave Himself for me! " " It rings like marriage bells in the heart! Not all the harps of heaven can sound out sweeter music than this, when the Holy Spirit speaks it to my soul, ' The Son of God, who loved me, and gave Himself for me.' " That is the grateful sentiment of a strong man, and these are all strong men, giants along the pilgrim way, and they never attempt to denude their piety of emotion or to de-personalise their religious life. They are great in the use of the pronouns, and great in the flow of tender yearning and desire, and their reason is all the more masculine, and their will is all the more massive because they do not deny the native rights of the heart. And all I wish to add is this, let us beware lest, in a healthy recoil from a wishy-washy sentimentalism, which pays little homage to the reason, we too " enter into life maimed," by adopting a desiccated rationalism, which dries up the very sap of piety, and drains away that fine emotion which is absolutely requisite to the finer issues of our faith.

Now turn to the apostle's personal glorying in the ministry of redemption. " He loved me, and gave Himself for me." And what was the purpose of the Lord's redemption? Humanity lay in a dire and awful bondage. There was the fearful appetite for sin. There was the relentless claim of violated law. There was the nemesis of guilt. There was the power of the devil. There was the clutch of superstition. And there was death and the fear of death. That was the bondage. And the Lover loved the bondslave, and the glorious crusade of the Lover was by love to bring "deliverance to the captive, and the opening of the prison to them that are bound." "He *loved*." Just there a false sentiment is born. Now love is holy. At the very heart of infinite love is incorruptible holiness, and in that innermost holiness lie the purpose and promise of our redemption. "O give thanks at the remembrance of His holiness!" But it is just here that false sentiment is born — that mawkish, effeminate, relaxing sentiment from which strong men recoil. There is a sentimentalism which bows before no shrine of virgin flame, and its morals are always lackadaisical, and its scheme of redemption is always cheap. It conceives love as a pretty rainbow, and not as "a rainbow round about the throne." It gathers a handful of flowers on the lower slopes of the mountains, but never ranges above the snow-line, amid the awe-inspiring, breath-gripping solitudes of the eternal snows. Yes, that is the obtrusive contrast between sentiment and sentimentalism. Sentimentalism is born among the flowers: a noble sentiment is born among the snows. Sentimentalism is born among graces: sentiment is born amid grace. Sentimentalism moves easily among kindnesses: sentiment moves wonderingly amid holiness. And therefore, I say, sentimentalism is inherently mawkish, while true sentiment is inherently austere. Sentimentalism takes liberties, while "the fear of the Lord is clean." When, therefore, I hear the evangel, "He loved me," I know that the glorious ministry is born of holiness: love is holiness in exercise, it is holiness in gracious movement, it is "a river of water of life proceeding out of the throne of God and

the Lamb." Our Lover is holy, and holy is His love.
"He loved me!" — the unholy and the unclean.

And because love is holy, love is inconceivably *sensi-tive*. The unhallowed is the insensitive, for sin is ever the minister of benumbment. Yes, the unclean makes the moral powers numb, and after every sin the sensitiveness is dulled, and life's responsiveness impaired. The gradient of purity is also the gradient of feeling: they advance or retrograde with equal steps. And therefore it is impossible for us to realise, even remotely, the sensitiveness of holiness, and therefore, again, our Saviour's sorrows are inconceivable. "Was ever sorrow like unto my sorrow?" "He trod the winepress alone." Holy love is infinitely sensitive, and "He loved me, and gave Himself for me."

And because holy love is sensitive, holy love is *re-demptive*. Holiness is ever positive and aggressive seeking by its own "consuming fire" to burn the hateful germs of sin. We may test our growth in holiness, not by our cloistered recoil from uncleanness, but by our positive action upon it. Holiness is not secretive, exclusive, but sanative and redemptive. It takes live coals from its altar-fires wherewith to purge the lips of the defiled. A negative holiness is as monstrous as a square circle, or a heatless fire. "He shall baptise you with the Holy Ghost and with fire, and ye shall be. . . ." Which just means this: holy love shall be an eager servant in the ministry of a positive redemption. And so "He loved me," He saw me in my low estate, and in His holiness He sought my holiness and my everlasting peace.

"He loved me, and *He gave Himself for me*." For holy, sensitive, redemptive love must of necessity be sacrificial. It is the very genius of holiness to be superlative, and in its sacrificial ministry it sacrifices self. "*He gave Himself for me!*" Will my readers wonder if I say that John Calvin, in his marvellous exposition of this epistle, devotes only half-a-dozen lines to an attempted interpretation of this phrase? And what is the reason? Why, this. That the great theologian lays down his pen in glorious, but overwhelming and impotent bewilderment! "No words," he says, "can properly express what this means; for who can find language to declare the excellency of the Son of God?" And so, I say, he just lays down his pen, and contemplates the glory in speechless wonder! "He gave Himself for me!" He endued Himself with the robe of flesh, He entered the house of bondage, He took upon Him the form of a bondslave that He might set the bondslave free. He walked the pilgrim path of limitation, the path of sorrow and temptation; face to face He met the devil, face to face He met "the terror feared of man," becoming "obedient unto death, even the death of the cross." "He gave Himself for me!" And in that holy sacrifice of love the holy law of God received perfect obedience, the violated law of God received a holy satisfaction, the sovereignty of the devil was smitten and overthrown, boastful death lost its sting, and the omnivorous grave its victory! "O death, where is thy sting? O grave, where is thy victory?" And *He* did it all, did it all! "Wilt thou bring *thy* cowl, thy shaven crown, thy chastity, thy purity, thy

works, thy merits? " He did it all! Says Luther,
" Paul had nothing in his mouth but Christ."

> "Nothing in my hands I bring,
> Simply to Thy cross I cling."

" He loved me and gave Himself for me." Such is
the passion of redemption.

Now let me pass to the secret of appropriation.
" *That life which I now live I live in faith, the faith
which is in the Son of God.*" And so the virtues of
the love-sacrifice are to become mine by faith, for by
faith I become incorporated with the triumphant Lord.
Yes, but what is faith? It is not the deliberate blinding of the judgment. It is not tremulous movement in
a small, fusty room, in which the casement window is
studiously kept shuttered, and in which we make a pious
vow never to open the lattice, and let in the morning
light and air. Now is faith the dethronement of the
reason, and the coronation of caprice? It is not " the
shutting of the eyes," and " the opening of the mouth,"
in unillumined expectation. Faith is reasonable dealing
in reasonable things. Faith is in the science of religion what experiment is in the science of matter. Faith
is reasonable experiment with the glorious hypotheses of
Christ. We begin with hypotheses, we discover truth.
But in the Christian religion all the hypotheses centre
round about the Saviour Himself, and therefore personal faith is personal dealing with Christ, faith is trust,
experiment is communion, exploration is by consecration,
knowledge is by homage; we lose our life and we find it
again in our Lord. Faith, therefore, is not finally men-

tal, or emotional, but volitional. Faith is ultimately an act of the will: it is the personal surrender of the life to the governance of the Saviourhood of Christ. It is the human side of the marriage-covenant between the Lamb and the Lamb's bride. Faith is the human end of the ministry which establishes union between the soul and its Lord. "We are justified by faith." "That life which I now live I live in faith, the faith which is in the Son of God, who loved me and gave Himself for me." Such is the secret of appropriation.

So far for the passion of redemption, and the secret of appropriation: and now, thirdly, the wonders of re-creation. What are to be the issues of the union, according to the teachings of my text? First of all, there is to be a certain *mortification:* "I am crucified with Christ." "The apostle speaketh," says one who is greatly at home in the affairs of the heart, "of that high crucifying, whereby sin, the devil and death are crucified in Christ, and not in me. . . . But I, believing in Christ, am by faith crucified also with Christ, so that all these things are crucified and dead unto me." Ay, and that not fictionally, but in sober and most literal truth. One of the gifts of redemption is a certain dead-ness; there is a dead side to a true believer: on that side, while he believes, his senses do not operate, and he offers no response. Have I not seen it scores upon scores of times? Have I not seen a believer, who by belief has become one with Christ, and who has become dead to the old baneful world of haunting guilt? Did I not hear one say, who had revelled forty years in sin, and who had become united with the Lord, that that forty-year-old man was dead, "crucified with Christ," and if any accusing day should shake a threatening finger at him, he would laugh in triumph, the finger was pointed at the dead, for that particular man " was crucified, dead and buried, and his life was hid with Christ in God! " And have I not seen a believer, who by belief has become one with Christ, and who has become dead to the insidious fascination of a glittering and destructive world? " Good-bye, proud world, I'm going home! " And have I not seen a believer, who by belief has become one with Christ, and who has become dead to death, and in death has exulted in " the power of an endless life." Oh, yes, one of the primary gifts of grace is the gift of deadness — deadness to the threat of yesterday, deadness to the fear of tomorrow, deadness to the frown of the immediate circumstance, and deadness to majestic death itself! " The last enemy that shall be destroyed is death." *I have been crucified with Christ." " I died.*

But there are other fruits of the union which is humanly established by faith in Christ. " I have been crucified with Christ " : mortification; *yet I live* " : vitalisation! "If we died with Him, we shall also live with Him! " The gift of deadness is the companion gift of vitality. " Everything shall live whither the river cometh." Dormant powers shall be aroused and shall troop forth out of their graves, powers of holy perception, and holy desire, and holy sympathy, and holy faculty for service. And old powers shall be renewed, and they shall be like anaemic weaklings who have attained a boisterous vitality. Our powers are far from their best until they become united to Christ. I saw a bit of edelweiss the other day growing in a garden in one of our suburbs; but it had to be labelled, it was so unlike its masculine kinsman gripping the desolate precipices of the lofty Alps. Ay, you must see the edelweiss at home! And if we want to see what love really is, and will, and conscience, and chivalry, we must see them at home, in their native clime, rooted and grounded in the life and love of the eternal Lord. " In Christ shall all be made alive."

" I have been crucified with Christ: yet I live: *and yet no longer I, but Christ . . . !* " So that is where we arrive. Mortification by Christ, vitalisation in Christ, *the manifestation of Christ.* " I live, yet no longer I." What is that but the suppression of the ego? Would it not be better to say, What is that but the conversion and transfiguration of the ego, and the emergence of the Lord? " No longer I, Christ liveth in me! " The Lord who pervades the life also dominates it. " The life which I now live in the flesh " reveals His power and His glory. He takes my humble affairs and He uses them as the shrine of His own Presence, the lampstand for His own eternal light. The life in the home, in the market, in the school, in the senate, in the closet, in the polling-booth, — the entire circuit of that life " which I now live in the flesh," " I live in faith! " " I live, yet no longer I, but Christ liveth in me." That is the Christian ideal, and that is the Christian possibility, however pitiably remote we may be from its attainment. Yes, that is the ideal, that Christ lives again in me, that my activities are the motions of my

Lord; that in me He faces again the Pharisee, in me He denounces again the oppressor of "the poor and him that hath no helper," in me He ministers again to the hungry, the paralysed, and the fever-stricken, and in me He champions again the cause of the Magdalene and the little child. " I live, yet no longer I, but *Christ*." Men shall gaze upon the issues of the life, and say, "It is the Lord! " and they shall glorify our Father which is in heaven.

II.

PROCRASTINATION

" When I have a convenient season, I will call thee unto me." Acts 24:25.

WE are to think this morning about the homely and familiar matter of procrastination. Instead of letting our thoughts dwell upon that abstract noun let us from the beginning have in our mind's eye a concrete picture of the life of Paul. Paul had been mobbed and nearly killed by his fellow-countrymen in Jerusalem, and, saved only by the intervention of the Roman soldiery, he soon found himself in prison in Caesarea, where he had been taken to escape lynching. There Felix, the governor, was alike his jailer and his judge. One night when the governor's wife, Drusilla, wished to hear and see this tempestuous and troublesome Jew, Felix had Paul brought before him, and allowed him freedom to speak. One might have thought that Paul's spirit would have been tamed by his perilous experience; but Paul was always like a fire that is not blown out but fanned into a fierce heat when the hard winds blow. Let the twenty-fourth chapter of the book of Acts tell us the simple narrative: "After certain days, Felix came with Drusilla, his wife, who was a Jewess, and sent for Paul, and heard him concerning his faith in Christ Jesus. And as he reasoned of righteousness, and self-control, and the judgment to come, Felix was terrified, and answered, Go thy way for this time; and when I have a convenient season, I will call thee unto me."

Felix is one of the most unlovely characters in Scripture, and all that we know of him outside of Scripture simply deepens our distaste for him. Yet it is apparent from this experience of his with Paul that like all the rest of us he was a strange combination of good and bad, that deep in his heart he had chords that the fine, strong fingers of a personality like Paul persuasively could play upon. Bad as he was, let us remember that there was one time when he heard the Gospel of Jesus and was stirred by it, when he heard great words about righteousness and self-control, and felt their appeal, when he looked upon his life and the end to which it was tending, and shrank back from it. He was not all bad.

This morning we are going to think of the way he dealt with this significant hour with the apostle. You will notice that he was not abusive and discourteous; he was not blasphemous and sceptical. He merely procrastinated. He simply postponed decision; he politely waived the matter aside, and said, "When I have a convenient season, I will call thee unto me." And so he lost the supreme opportunity of his life.

Is it not so that we are continually making failures of our lives? Here in this church, where through another winter we have so repeatedly presented appeals for the Master, for the type and quality of spirit which He represents, for the concrete opportunities of service which His cause offers, one does not suspect that there has been much brusque and deliberate rejection, much scornful and contemptuous scepticism; but one does suspect that among all the people who have gathered here there must be a great deal of procrastination. It is so popular a method of avoidance. It can be indulged in so easily and without offense. How many times in this church do you suppose these words have in effect been spoken in the hearts of men: " Go thy way for this time; and when I have a convenient season, I will call thee unto me? "

We are all perfectly familiar with this habit of procrastination in practical details. We do not decide not to answer a letter from a friend. We simply postpone answering it. We take it up, and dally with it, and lay it aside for a more convenient time. We do not decide not to make a call that ought to be made. We merely postpone making it. We let the days and weeks pass; and ever, as we postpone it, it becomes easier to postpone it still, until, at last, the call is never made at all. We never decide not to hear the best music and read the best books. We merely defer doing so. We comfort our consciences by saying: "Sometime we will see this or hear that." And we never decide not to pay serious attention to the religious education of our children. We simply put it off; we refer it to this nebulous, convenient tomorrow when all letters are going to be answered, all calls made, all privileges enjoyed, and all duties done. With this popular habit of procrastination we are perfectly familiar.

But surely it is not so small and trivial a matter as too frequently we are tempted to suppose. Leonardo da Vinci's picture of the Last Supper was spoiled by a single broken tile through which the rain poured down across the face of Christ. So great a picture to be spoiled by so small a thing! Yet after many years of watching folk from the vantage point of the ministry, I am sure that many lives are spoiled in that way, and that the broken tile is the habit of procrastination.

Pick up the words of Felix this morning, one of the classic utterances of a confirmed procrastinator, and look into them until, as in a mirror, they reveal us to ourselves.

First of all, how full of hope they are! Felix is counting on the future. "A more convenient season," he says politely to Paul as he bids him good-night; and at once we are aware that procrastination is the perversion of something good. It is the abuse of hope. It is the misuse of tomorrow. Now, tomorrow is one of God's best gifts to men. The animals do not possess it. They have only today, — their yesterdays dim and vague, their tomorrows prepared for by instinct, but not by expectation, — but man has yesterday and today and tomorrow. How utterly bereft we all should be without that backreach of memory and that outreach of hope! If today the clouds overspread our sky, tomorrow the sun may shine again. If today sickness has invaded our homes, tomorrow health may come back once more. If today our business is vexatious and troublesome, tomorrow may see the turning of the tide that will bring back the better times. If today our temptations seem insupportable, tomorrow we may find spiritual power to overcome. And if today we are cast down by the weariness and tragedy of this war-rent mankind, we turn to a prophet to encourage us about tomorrow: " My own hope is, a sun will pierce the thickest cloud earth ever stretched." We should all be lost without tomorrow, for in hope we are saved.

But here, as always, the perversion of the best is the worst, and the perversion of tomorrow is procrastination. For we keep putting off until tomorrow the enjoyment of privileges and the use of opportunities that we ought to rejoice in today. I suspect that we ministers are partly responsible for this very attitude against which I speak. For continually we plead for ideals we are sometime to realize but have not yet attained; we urge gains in personal and social life that are sometime to be achieved, but are not yet achieved. We fill in the picture of tomorrow with blessings to be enjoyed, ideals to be attained, until the upshot may be that we draw the thought of our people away from what they have today to what they may have tomorrow. Today in our preaching becomes too often something to be overpassed and outgrown, but tomorrow is the home of fulfilled ideals. There is, however, a serious fallacy in this. We need continually to be reminded not simply of what we may have sometime, but of what we do have today.

It is a shame to see a man running across his todays as a boy runs a race, with his eyes tightly fixed upon the far goal, thinking only of what lies ahead. But many men do so run their lives. "Tomorrow," they cry, while all the time today presents them privileges and blessings that they run past, not seeing.

"Felix, come and enjoy the sunset," and Felix says: "Tomorrow." But tomorrow the sunset will not be one whit more beautiful than it is today if we have eyes to see it.

"Felix, let us rejoice in friendship"; and Felix says, "Tomorrow." But friends will be not one bit more beautiful than they are today if we have eyes to see and hearts to understand.

"Felix, let us grow up with our children, and even here on earth gain a foretaste of heaven which a true home affords." And Felix says, "Tomorrow." But your children will not be one bit more fascinating in their youthful companionship tomorrow than they are today; and you may say "Tomorrow" too long, until there are no children to grow up with in your home at all.

"Felix, let us enter into the sustaining fellowship of Christ, see life from His height, and live in His spirit"; and Felix says, "Tomorrow." But Christ will not be one whit more gracious and redeeming tomorrow than He is today.

My friends, after all, today is all we actually do possess. Yesterday is gone, and tomorrow is not yet here; and procrastination is a deadly habit of blinding one's eyes to the opportunities and privileges we have in our hands and dreaming of something that sometime we may have. "Carpe diem," cried the old Latins, "Seize the day."

There are many of us who do not learn this significant lesson until we learn it in the hardest of all ways; we lose something that we have had in our possession a long time, too little appreciated; and then we wake up to wish above all things that we might have it back again. So an old man may look back upon the strength of youth that once he had. What a splendid time it was when he awoke each morning with power sufficient for his tasks, and went out to work with joy! Why did he not appreciate it more when he had it, and get more out of it? Often a man feels so about his friends when they are gone. What tonic, refreshing spirits they were! Why did he not take more advantage of the fine boon of their fellowship when he had the chance? So, oftentimes, mothers feel about their children. They were so beautiful! Why did they leave them so much with others and live with them so little when they had a chance?

So, continually we are waking up to discover, only when we have lost them, that for years we have had life's choicest privileges within our grasp; for years we have been saying, "Tomorrow," while each today was filled with unrealized possibilities. You will know where this applies to you. I am sure it does apply, for I am sure that every one of us has in his possession now relationships, blessings, opportunities, privileges, concerning which after each is gone, he will say, "Why did I not make more of it while I had it?" My friends, it will not do to go on postponing everything until tomorrow. If a man is going to live a fine, rich, radiant, and joyful Christian life, it were better to begin today.

Once more pick up these words of Felix and look at them. "A convenient season," he says to Paul, and at once we are aware that he doesn't think that he is deciding the question that Paul has raised. He thinks that he has postponed the decision, but he hasn't. For indecisive procrastination is one of the most conclusive methods of decision that mankind knows. Now, the reason for this is perfectly simple. Life's processes do not call a halt simply because we have not made up our minds. If here in New York City or in the country round about you have this spring a garden-plot, you may suppose that you have three choices; either to have flowers, or to have weeds, or to be hesitant, uncertain, indecisive. But in fact you have only two choices. If you choose flowers, you may have them; but if you decide to be indecisive, nature will decide for you. You will have weeds. The processes of God's eternal universe do not stop to wait for us to make up our minds.

Now, life continually is facing us with these enforced decisions, where to endeavor to escape decision by procrastination is utter futility. For procrastination is irretrievable decision. Reach down into life at random, anywhere, and you will find illustrations in plenty. Shall we try to stop the starvation of the Chinese? is a question that has been facing us all these winter and spring months. Do you say you will wait for a more convenient season to make up your mind? You may as well say that you will not help them at all. For the processes of starvation do not cease until you decide. They still stalk their ghastly way through the Celestial Land, and take their toll of thousands and tens of thousands every day. To be indecisive is not to be indecisive. It is one of the most conclusive, fatal, irretrievable decisions you can make.

Or come in to a more homely episode. You see a purse dropped in the street and you see the one who dropped it. You may suppose that you have three choices: either to be honest and return it, be dishonest and keep it, or be indecisive, uncertain. But you have only two choices. If you decide to be indecisive, the processes of life will not wait for you. The crowds will surge in between you and the purse's owner, and the opportunity of being honest which was yours for a moment will vanish; and, while you yourself will not decide, life will have decided for you and leave you standing there, dishonest.

Or, once more, let your imagination reach out to the most stupendous problem in the world today, the avoidance of war. Some people think we have three choices: either to make a united stand in favor of disarmament, to save the world from this intolerable burden of taxation for war that is breaking the back of our civilization; or to refuse to do that and to plunge deliberately into huge competition in armament in preparation for another war; or to be indecisive, to dally and defer, to procrastinate and put off. But as a matter of fact we have only two choices. The processes of life are not waiting — God pity us! — for us to make up our minds. We are like ships upon a sea where to drift means wreck as certainly as though with full deliberation we steered toward the rocks. A little more indecisiveness, uncertainty, procrastination, a little more folding of the hands and crying, " Tomorrow," and it will be decided. We shall have another war.

In the same class with those illustrative instances lies that question on which Felix tried to postpone decision, the question of a righteous, self-controlled, and Christian life. For see this one element that runs through all these illustrative cases. To make flowers grow means positive decision; to help starving Chinese means a deliberate act; to be honest in a crisis means a thrust of the will; to move toward disarmament means a resolute act of the public conscience. All great things cause positive decision. You cannot float them like a thistledown blowing in the wind. And being a Christian is a great thing. You cannot become a Christian in your sleep. You must make up your mind to do it. And if any Felix endeavors to be indecisive, he is not really indecisive. His life processes still go on without Christ because he has not positively decided for Christ.

No earnest minister could speak on such a theme without thinking of the young men and women here who, it may be, have been in attendance on these morning services all this winter past, and now, as school or college closes, go to their homes, or, it may be, begin their business or professional careers. I speak to some of you as though I might never have the chance to speak to you again. No one would urge you to choose something that you do not understand or that you do not believe. But if you have caught at all the emphasis of this pulpit, you must see how little we care here about those sectarian peccadillos that have marred the church, and the theological peculiarities that have disfigured her serious thought; you must have seen how earnestly we have pressed our emphasis back to that central matter, the spirit of Jesus, His filial sacrificial passion for the coming of the kingdom of righteousness upon the earth, the faith that empowered Him, the hope that sustained Him, the character that was His crown and glory. You haven't three choices about that. You have two choices. You may glorify your life if you will by having Him for the Master of your soul. But if you try to be indecisive, you are not indecisive; you are missing Him; you are missing Him as thoroughly as though you said, " No " to Him. For you will go out to live a life not mastered by His positive faiths, not dedicated to His positive cause.

As one thinks of this refusal through procrastination, he sees how many men are living in just this attitude. For there are multitudes of people to whose hearts the highest impulses are not strange at all, who again and again have risen to the appeal of Jesus like waves that almost come to their crest, but not quite; they never quite break into the white foam of a finished billow; but they rise and sink, rise and sink, forever moving, but moving nowhere, forever promising, but never consummated. How futile is a life like that in any realm! In literature Coleridge was the consummate example of procrastination. He projected more poems, more essays, more lectures, than any other man that ever lived; but he finished almost nothing — a few things like " The Ancient Mariner," but not much else. He planned everything, but he postponed work on anything. You pick up a page, and read,

> " In Xanadu did Kubla Khan
> A stately pleasure-dome decree:
> Where Alph, the sacred river, ran
> Through caverns measureless to man
> Down to a sunless sea."

You say, " This is fascinating." But the trouble is, that is about all there is of it. He never finished it. It was a passing impulse. He never made up his mind to write it through. He was an animated prospectus, full of deferred plans.

But there are many of us who have no business to laugh at him. In a far more deep and important matter than writing poems, we are living that kind of a life. Again and again we have felt the appeal of Christ. Again and again we have felt the lure of an open, decisive, consistent Christian life in a generation when open, decisive, and consistent Christian lives are more needed than anything else; but we are still uncertain, irresolute, procrastinating. I wish there were one here this morning who would cease the refusal of the highest through procrastination, who would say, " As for me, now, now is the accepted time, and now is the day of salvation."

Just once more pick up these words of Felix and look at them. " A convenient season," he says politely and cheerfully to Paul as he bids him good-night, and you perceive at once that he confidently thinks that there will be a convenient season. He has not deeply perceived that serious truth which runs through all human life, that there is such a thing as being too late. Procrastination a small fault? No, not in a universe where some things have to be done on time if they are going to be done at all. Says the tree in April, "I will not put forth my leaves now — in May"; and in May the tree says, "A more convenient season — June." But it would better take care. If leaves are not forthcoming in April or May or June, it is getting late. July is no time for leaves to come, and August is almost hopeless, and September is quite too late. He must have blind eyes who cannot see that truth running all through human life, a serious truth to which no cheap and easy optimism ought ever to blind our sight.

The truth is inherent in the very fact of growing up from youth to age. What a fairyland of possibilities youth is! Listen to this lad talking. He is not sure, he says, yet, whether he is to be a civil engineer, or a business man, or a lawyer, or a professional aviator; and he thinks he might be a minister. And, when he talks to you like that, what is more, you must listen to him seriously. He may be any one of them. The doors are all open. He is young. But we who have reached maturity have all these years been listening to a sound with which we are perfectly familiar, the sound of shutting doors. The range of our possible choices has been narrowing down. We know well enough that there are some things on this earth we never can do now. It is too late. Happy the man who has chosen right! Happy the man who has not put off too long doing something that he wanted to do very much indeed.

Alongside this fact of the inevitable passage of the years, the possibility of being too late is accentuated by the companion fact of habit. There may have been a time when you could straighten out the down-town streets of Boston, when they were meandering cow-paths along the shores of Massachusetts Bay, but it is too late now. They have been widened into streets and set in asphalt, and curbed in stone, and the life of the metropolis has immovably solidified itself around them. It is too late. So is the set of habit in the life of man.

It is no small matter, then, to say to young men and women on their fluid years of choice that they would better make the decision that concerns the deep interests of their spiritual life. For Felix is not ancient character alone. He has had a multitude of reincarnations. Edgar Allan Poe was another Felix. He died as a result of a drunken night's revel in a saloon in Baltimore. You say he was bad? A man cannot content himself in speaking of such a man by saying, " He is bad." Look upon that brutal, drunken death, and think of what he wrote:

" For the moon never beams without bringing me dreams
  Of the beautiful Annabel Lee,
 And the stars never rise but I feel the bright eyes
  Of the beautiful Annabel Lee;
 And so, all the night-tide, I lie down by the side
 Of my darling — my darling — my life and my bride,
  In the sepulchre there by the sea,
  In her tomb by the sounding sea."

Surely, men who write like that are not all bad. There are harbours in the world where the harbour bar is so high that it never can be passed at low tide; so the ships wait for the high tide that they may enter in. So are the souls of men. Think of the flood tides, then, that a man like Edgar Allan Poe must have had when the sky called to the deep, and in his heart there were voices speaking, like Paul before Felix, about righteousness and self-control and judgment to come. But he would not decide! Up and down, up and down, outside the harbour bar he sailed his craft, irresolute, procrastinating, till the tide went out, and then it was too late.

And this possibility of being too late is of course accentuated, so far as this earth is concerned, by death. I do not know whether that impresses me more when I think of my own death or when I think of the death of my friends. For when death comes, it does come very suddenly. Ah, if you have anybody to love, you would better love him now. If you have little children to be brought up in the spirit of Jesus, you would better do it now. If you have quarrelled with some one with whom in your deepest heart you did not mean to quarrel, you would better make it right now. If you have any contributions that you can make to build here a juster, kindlier world for our humanity, you would better make it now. And if you know a Lord whose service is perfect freedom, a Saviour whose love is wider than the measure of man's mind, you would better choose Him now.

My young friends, there are three great choices that

a man makes in his experience: First, his vocation, what
he will do with his life; second, his marriage, who will
be the mother of his children; and third, his faith, who
shall be the guide of his soul. I think you know that
Jesus Christ has a right to that place. Then put Him
there — not tomorrow — *today*.

III.

RELIGION

Then they that feared the Lord spake often one with
another and the Lord hearkened and heard, and a book of
remembrance was written before him for them that feared
the Lord and that thought upon his name.

MALACHI 3:16

I SHOULD like to speak to you today of what religion
means to us and of what we mean by religion.

To one familiar with man's past life on earth religion in some form appears to be the most inalienable
endowment of the human race. However far back we
go we are never able to go back to a time when religion
was not. The oldest literary monuments of mankind,
the Rig Veda, the Upanishads, the Book of Genesis,
the most ancient cuneiform inscriptions of Babylon, the
Book of the Dead and the oldest inscriptions and texts
of Egypt, all are taken up with man's sense of the divine
and with his attempts to regulate his life by divine sanc-
tions. And in the remote and hoary past of our race,
where all literary monuments fail, ages before writing

was invented, where we have nothing but bones and sepulchres to guide us, in the ceremonial burials of these long-forgotten days, the weapons, the utensils, the untasted food placed beside the corpse still bear their mute testimony to man's glimmering faith in a life beyond death.

And as it is in the past, so is it when we descend the scale of humanity even to its lowest, most primitive representatives. As far as I am aware no people has yet been discovered without its mythology, its religious tabus, its sense of the divine. Lately, I have been reading a volume of Marshall Jones' great *Mythology of All Races*, the volume which deals with the primitive races of Africa, including the Pygmies, and I find that even these diminutive and darkened minds have not escaped the universal spell. Myths of creation and of the origin of man, good and evil spirits, expectation of life after death, responsibility to an unseen power, even some conception of a Most High God, have controlled their lives as they have controlled the lives of other men.

The possession of religion is the most universal and catholic fact we can point to in man, a fact which apparently man did not make, but which has made man, and the most amazing aspect of this fact is that it has endured so long and that it has triumphed over so many vicissitudes. Existing long before science and philosophy were thought of, it has been able not merely to adjust itself to, but to inspire the highest science and philosophy so that no interpretation of Nature or of life can satisfy our minds which is not a religious interpretation. Beginning with the crudest, ugliest representations and symbols, it has created the only perfect works of art, the only unsurpassable monuments of architecture, the music which most perfectly expresses the spiritual hopes and aspirations of man. Dealing almost exclusively with the unseen and the imponderable, with those very things which might seem the most unreal, the most impractical and useless, this religious and spiritual belief has done man more practical good than all his other knowledge and beliefs put together, has done him so much good that without this faith in God and the soul all his other knowledge and beliefs have not been able to make man either good or happy. Always contradicted, always doubted, always apparently about to be overthrown, out of all these conflicts with reason, with fanaticism, with the violence of tyrants, religion has risen again, apparently only purified and strengthened, to make its new appeal, or to resume its ancient sway over the human heart. So it spans the history of mankind as the rainbow spans the verge of the cataract apparently always about to be swept away by the impetuous waters, yet in some mysterious way always sustained by them, always glorifying them.

When I think of religion I think first of Jesus Christ. To us He is religion, at least all that is perfect in religion. The personality of the Redeemer, His thought, His sayings in regard to life, His sympathy with sorrow, His attitude toward disease, His love for children and for sinners, His conception of the Kingdom of God, the motives which led Him to lay down His life, His death on the cross, His resurrection — all those human and divine things which shine in the Gospels — are worth far more to me and I esteem them of infinitely greater religious value than the metaphysical subtleties and mumbling, which work no miracle and which speak to no heart, by which men have tried to explain Him. I consider the days and the years I have spent in the study of Him the happiest days and years of my life. When I hear men criticize and belittle Him, or rather the ideas they falsely ascribe to Him, I say, if I have the opportunity, "Ah! if you really knew."

When I speak thus I am not unmindful of the great debt of gratitude we owe to some of the other religious teachers of mankind, but there is one thought of Christ's which if we wish to tell the truth we must admit that we find nowhere else. One clear conception of Jesus in regard to the use of life separates His religion from all the religions of the world, and gives to Christianity its enormous potential energy and its practical social value as a religion of redemption. That is Christ's conception of life as active service, as a ministry of love and compassion, the conquest of the evil of this world by the love and goodness of His followers, the thought of sacrifice, not to please God, as if God derived satisfaction from our suffering, but to save and help men.

This thought of redemption summed up in the glorious phrase, "The Kingdom of God," belongs wholly to Jesus. Buddha conceived of redemption as the annihilation of self. Neither Moses, nor Zoroaster, nor Mohammed, nor Confucius, nor the prophets ever expressed the meaning and opportunity of life in these terms. The thought of life as a service of love and the service of God as effected through the service of men is a thought wholly original to Jesus. As far as this disposition is my disposition and day by day I serve my fellow men according to my strength, ability and opportunity, in the humblest things as well as in the highest, I am Christ's and a member of the Kingdom of God. As far as I put this thought far from me and am content to live merely for myself, my honor and glory, my pleasures, my vices, I have no part nor lot in Christ's cause and no right to call myself by His name.

In order to make this very plain to us Jesus uttered one of His greatest sayings, His story of the Last Judgment. It is by this principle and by this only that He judges the worth of every life. The saved and blessed persons whom He welcomes to His Father's Kingdom are those who did what they could and who served their fellow men by giving food to the hungry, drink to the thirsty, clothing to the naked, care to the sick, sympathy and human companionship to the lonely prisoner. Those whom He pronounced accursed and from whom He shudderingly withdraws Himself He condemns not for what they had done, not for their crimes and the weaknesses of their human natures but for what they had left undone, for their selfishness, their cold-heartedness, their uselessness, their cruel neglect.

Does anywhere in the world Christ's judgment of life stand in such direct opposition to the judgment of society? How our hypocritical censors of life, our Scribes and Pharisees, would like to instruct Christ in regard to these matters and to prove to Him that He did not and could not mean what He said. As if to forestall them, He uttered His judgment of life in words which cannot be silenced and which cannot be explained away.

Pitifully, half-heartedly as this principle has been accepted and acted on, what we have done in obedience to this view of the purpose of life is the cause of most of the superiority and nobility Christian nations possess. Compare our achievement with that of nations to which this view of life is unknown and you will perceive there is a difference.

Prayer I count a great element of religion. Indeed without prayer I do not see how personal religion can long go on. In prayer the soul is awake, the soul speaks. In true prayer that deep, mysterious thing within us, that person of light, served by the senses, surrounded by knowledge, that thing which beyond all other things we account ourself, turns to the Universal Soul from which it sprang and tries to unite itself to God. From that contact, according to its frequency and depth and intensity, light and joy and the renewal of our vitality, peace, courage and consolation are poured into us. It is not as if our little soul, like a water drop is lost in the immensity of God. At times, as the mystics say, it is as if the whole ocean of God's being were poured into the water drop.

To all men at times prayer is so natural that they pray spontaneously. They cry out to God hardly knowing that they have cried. In moments of great emergency, great sorrow, great danger, we pray because we cannot help praying. This is because at such times the soul must utter itself and make its appeal to the source of its

life. Among the men and women I have known I cannot remember one who I did not believe possessed a soul.
What this soul is, who can say?   In itself we call it
something spiritual to distinguish it from intellect,
though that explains nothing. In its relation to reality, it
is more immediate, more intuitive, more affectionate,
more personal, more living than the processes and ap-
proximations of reason. Through our study of the subconscious we have explored more than one room of the
soul's many mansions. On the one side this subconscious mind controls all the marvelous processes of our
physical life. On the other it may rise to the divinations
and intuitions of genius.

Even in the case of the insane, the idiotic, the im-
becile, the absence of manifestation of all spiritual life
is no proof that the soul has perished, any more than the
inability of an organist to play a fugue of Bach on a
broken and ruined instrument is proof that he is a fool.
Perhaps, under these sad circumstances, even while the
body is living the soul is able to disengage itself from the
diseased or injured brain and to find a sweeter and pleas-
anter abode for itself than our insane asylums. This
may seem foolish to you, but it does not seem so to
Professor Schiller, a great teacher of philosophy in
Oxford University.

Suppose that what I believe to be true, is true. Suppose that this massive material universe which reason has
so completely dissolved into energy and motion, is but
one aspect of reality, the aspect which is presented to our
senses and through our senses to our minds, but that
there is also another aspect. Behind this body or these

worlds of bodies there is a soul, that is to say a creative purpose, a living presence, love, truth, beauty, power. On the one side all is massive, apparently dead, cold, purposeless. On the other side all is living, warm, purposeful. Would not our dim perception of this reality, our experience of what has come to us from the unseen and from our spiritual communion with God, account for the undying power of religion, the miracles religion has wrought, and also for its independence of, and relative indifference to, rational explanations of it all? It is not explanations we want, or even proofs of the existence of God, could these be given to us. It is contact with the divine, the seeking of God's face, letting our hearts go forth to God and communion with Him in the secret places. In this search for God, if men had found nothing, would they have sought so long? The most primitive peoples may have been endowed with psychic perceptions which we have largely lost, though some still possess them. They found in the spiritual world something real which they interpreted in terms of their simple experience as beings like themselves. We also have derived from that world our spiritual life which we interpret in the terms of science and philosophy and purer religion. To the great religious teachers of mankind, above all to the Lord Jesus, the eternal world of power stood open and He expected it at any time to reveal itself and to take possession of this world. In this sense the Kingdom of God some day will certainly come. It may come to any generation. On these personal experiences of the great spiritual teachers of mankind, mankind has founded its religions. Is not this the most probable explanation both of the origin and of the deathless power of religion? There is a reality which we apprehend not through our senses but through our souls and which our minds interpret as they can in terms of experience. Deny this reality as much as you please, it reveals itself again in a higher, more convincing form. The conscious yielding of ourselves to this Reality, the willing identification of our souls with it, we call prayer.

Never, perhaps, in the history of the Church have the benefits of prayer received such general recognition as in our lifetime. Never, perhaps, have so many men prayed with so much faith. When we seek to estimate the tendencies of our times we must not fail to include prayer, a new and earnest desire to pray.

I wish I had time to speak of some of the minor things, if anything in religion can be called minor, which help to keep faith, hope and love alive in our breasts. Of these, of course, the souls of other men are the most important. It is because men discovered divine things in the past that we believe in them today. Few of us would be able to make these discoveries ourselves. But we have a rich and glorious inheritance from the past, above all in the Bible, which no age, however youthful, can dispense with. Why is the world materially so rich today? Because we are living on the vast supplies of coal and iron, copper and oil and other things laid away for us by the rays of the sun millions of years ago. If we had to grow these things or to produce them in some way year by year, we should not be rich. We are simply living on the treasures of the past. So through the long ages, by struggle, by suffering, by spiritual genius and discovery, humanity has been amassing a spiritual capital which gives meaning to the generations as they pass and on which they can freely draw. There will never be another Jesus, there will never be another St. Paul, there will never be another sacred book like the Bible. The time for such a book is over.

Nor is it only the dead who minister to our spiritual life. In the sweetness of human affection, in the pure, poetic minds of children, in our deep and tender love for men and women, in an unexpected act of kindness, in a glance of affection, in our musings over our past lives, in our regrets for our failures and foolishness, in our desire to make the only atonement given to man — to do better — how frequently our feet stray into sacred places and we touch the divine. Love and memory, sorrow and hope, are the words of God to us on which, as Jesus said, man lives. They are like the bells of the old French legend, buried at the bottom of the sea, whose sweet notes rise trembling in our hearts from their infinite depths and fall on our spirits like voices from another world. "To live with joy and to die with better hope." This, as Cicero said, is the gift religion bestows upon us. When all is said, there is a difference between him that serveth God and him that serveth Him not.

GEORGE MacDONALD ON PREACHING

" I PROFESS myself a believer in preaching and consider that in so far as the Church of England has
ceased to be a preaching Church — and I don't call nine-
tenths of what goes by the name of it *preaching* — she
has forgotten a weighty part of her high calling. Of
course a man to whom no message has been personally
given has no right to take the place of a prophet, and
cannot save by more or less of simulation; but there is
room for teachers as well as prophets, and the more
need of teachers that the prophets are so few: and a
man might honestly be a clergyman who teaches his
people, though may possess none of the gifts of
prophecy."

. . . " Pray, what do you mean by prophecy? " said
Wingfold. " I mean what I take to be the sense in
which St. Paul uses the word — I mean the highest
kind of preaching. But I will come to the point prac-
tically: a man, I say, who does not feel in his soul that
he has something to tell his people should straightway
turn his energy to the providing of such food for them
as he finds feeds himself. In other words if he has
nothing new in his own treasures, let him bring something old out of another man's. " . . .

" Then do you intend that a man should make up his
sermons from the books he reads? "

" Yes, if he can do no better. But then I would
have him read — not with his sermon in his eye but
with his people in his heart. Men in business and pro-

fessions have so little time for reading and thinking —
and idle people have still less — that their means of
grace, as the theologians say, are confined to discipline
without nourishment, whereas their religion, if they have
any, is often from mere atrophy but a skeleton; and the
office of preaching is first of all to wake them up lest
their sleep turn to death; next to make them hungry;
and lastly, to supply that hunger."

THOMAS WINGFOLD, *Curate* Chap. XVI.

PROFESSOR F. NIEBERGALL ON THE PSY-CHOLOGY OF THE CONCLUSION

PROFESSOR NIEBERGALL in his *Wie predigen wir dem
modernen Menschen?* ("How shall we preach to
modern men?"), 2nd part, p. 133, gives wise counsel
to the preacher about the way in which the sermon should
be concluded. "One must save for the end such ideas
as call into play the mental organs which have the greatest endurance. Therefore one should use as little as
absolutely necessary such combinations and constructions
as require thought, since they find little reception in the
exhausted mind. Everyone knows, of course, that a
listener likes best to leave church and sermon in an
exalted mood. Therefore you should close with a call
to the emotions; that is, to the deepest life interests, such
as happiness, exaltation of life, the progress and thriving
of children and home, of the whole community; but
be sure you know how far you may go. Not everyone
has much interest in his nation, or in the whole of Chris-

tendum or in all humanity. One must know where the interest ceases with most listeners. A well-told, interesting anecdote may also be good as an ending, for it will call forth the last bit of attention. A picture, a comparison or a colorful painting, which may, for instance, present the contrast between good and bad conduct, has a certain effect and accompanies the hearer when he goes home. In the same manner a verse of song, or a quotation remains in the memory, either on account of pleasure in its form or on account of its spiritual meaning. But, especially, the ending must be short and should not repeat something already stated, since boredom is felt first where the hope of an approaching end rules the attention; for then disappointment and anger are felt to a great degree."

SELECTED BIBLIOGRAPHY

THE literature on preaching is large and much of it consists of repetition. The books mentioned below are chosen with a view to help beginners in pulpit work amid the complexities of modern life. One ancient treatise is still worth studying, Augustine's *De Doctrina Christiana*, Bk. IV. There are two English translations, one published by T. & T. Clark (Edinburgh), and the other by Mowbray (London).

PREACHING AS AN ART

W. J. Lyman, *Preaching in the New Age*; Roland C. Smith, *Preaching as a Fine Art*; E. C. Dargan, *The Art of Preaching in the Light of its History*; Fenelon, *Dialogues sur L'Eloquence*; C. R. Brown, *The Art of Preaching* (Lect. II).

THE PERSONALITY OF THE PREACHER

J. Brierley, *Studies of the Soul* (Chap. XXXIV, " The Soul in Preaching "); J. H. Jowett, *The Preacher, His Life and Work*; W. J. Tucker, *The Making and Unmaking of the Preacher*; A. S. Hoyt, *The Preacher: His Person, Message and Method*, (Pt. I); W. P. Merrill, *Freedom of the Preacher*, (Chap. II); J. Paterson Smythe, *The Preacher and His Sermon* (Lect. I); E. E. Jefferson, *Quiet Hints to Growing Preachers*.

PREPARATION FOR PREACHING

J. Black, *The Mystery of Preaching* (pp. 70–97); W. B. O'Dowd, *Preaching* (Chap. V); Slattery, *Present Day Preaching* (Chap. II).

TEXT AND THEME

O. S. Davis, *Principles of Preaching*; A. S. Hoyt, *The Work of Preaching* (Lects. IV, V); T. H. Pattison, *The Making of the Sermon* (pp. 19–140); J. O. Dykes, *The Christian Minister and His Duties* (Chap. XXII).

THE STRUCTURE OF THE SERMON

T. Marks, *Pedagogics of Preaching*; W. Boyd Carpenter, *Lectures on Preaching*; P. Brooks, *Lectures on Preaching* (Lects. IV, V); J. M. English, *For Pulpit and Platform* (Chap. IV); C. R. Brown, *The Art of Preaching* (Lect. III); A. Vinet, *Homilétique*, (Pt. II.) (Eng. translation by T. H. Skimmer); Garvie, *The Christian Preacher* (pp. 421–442).

THE PREACHER AS PROPHET AND TEACHER

R. F. Horton, *Verbum Dei*; C. D. Williams, *The Prophetic Ministry for To-day*; E. Herman, *Christianity and the New Age* (Pt. II); A. C. McGiffert, Article in Hibbert Journal July, 1920, *The Teaching Function of the Ministry*.

THE DELIVERY OF THE SERMON

A. Monod, *The Delivery of Sermons* (A lecture); M. Bautain, *The Art of Extempore Speaking*; H. Ford, *The Art of Extempore Preaching*; F. H. Kirkpatrick, *Public Speaking: A Natural Method*; J. Caird, *University Addresses* (pp. 332–359); S. S. Curry, *Vocal and Literary Interpretation of the Bible* (consult references in Index); J. Parker, *Ad Clerum* (Chap. IV); R. S. Stone, *Preaching without Notes*; G. J. Holyoake, *Public Speaking and Debate* (Chap. XXVI).

The Psychology of Preaching

H. W. Beecher, *Yale Lectures on Preaching* (First Series, Lect. V); C. S. Gardiner, *Psychology and Preaching*; J. S. Kennard, *Psychic Power in Preaching*; H. C. Miller, *The New Psychology and the Preacher*; J. A. Hadfield, *The Psychology of Power* (in Essays on *The Spirit*, edited by B. H. Streeter).

Qualities of Effective Preaching

J. H. Jowett, *Apostolic Optimism* (pp. 262–277); J. Black, *Mystery of Preaching* (pp. 98–123); J. Gowan, *Homiletics*, (Chap. X); J. Watson, *The Cure of Souls* (Chap. III); L. O. Brastow, *The Modern Pulpit* (Chap. III).

Date Due

DEC 20 '74			
FEB 10 '77			
FEB 11 '81			
SEP 15 '82			

Demco 38-297